A HOME IN THE HEART
The Story of Sandra Cisneros

A HOME IN THE HEART
The Story of Sandra Cisneros

Virginia Brackett

620 South Elm Street, Suite 223
Greensboro, North Carolina 27406
http://www.morganreynolds.com

A HOME IN THE HEART: THE STORY OF SANDRA CISNEROS

Copyright © 2005 by Virginia Brackett

Morgan Reynolds, Inc., 620 S. Elm St., Suite 223
Greensboro, North Carolina 27406 USA

Library of Congress Cataloging-in-Publication Data

Brackett, Virginia.
 A Home in the Heart : The Story of Sandra Cisneros / Virginia Brackett.
   p. cm. — (World writers)
 Includes bibliographical references and index.
 ISBN 1-931798-42-7 (library binding)
 1. Cisneros, Sandra—Juvenile literature. 2. Authors, American—20th century—Biography—Juvenile literature. 3. Mexican American authors—Biography—Juvenile literature. 4. Mexican American women—Biography—Juvenile literature. I. Title. II. Series.
 PS3553.I78Z58 2004
 818'.5409—dc22

                    2004008409

Printed in the United States of America
First Edition

Sandra Cisneros

Virginia Woolf

Edgar Allan Poe

Jane Addams

Isak Dinesen

H.P. Lovecraft

Gwendolyn Brooks

Richard Wright

Henry Wadsworth Longfellow

Nathaniel Hawthorne

Stephen Crane

F. Scott Fitzgerald

Langston Hughes

Washington Irving

Edgar Rice Burroughs

H.G. Wells

Sir Arthur Conan Doyle

Isaac Asimov

Bram Stoker

Mary Shelley

Jules Verne

Ida Tarbell

George Orwell

Mary Wollstonecraft

World Writers

For Kay, Nancy, and Bruce

Contents

Chapter One
Born into Two Cultures 11
Chapter Two
From Duckling to Swan 22
Chapter Three
Like Pearls on a Necklace 36
Chapter Four
Crossing Borders 46
Chapter Five
So Many Things Terrify 58
Chapter Six
Fierce Women 68
Chapter Seven
Writer and Activist 84
Chapter Eight
Keeping the Faith 97

Timeline 116
Sources 118
Bibliography 125
Index 127

Sandra Cisneros
(Photograph courtesy of John Dyer, © John Dyer, 2005.)

Chapter One

Born into Two Cultures

The University of Iowa Writers' Workshop is one of the most prestigious graduate programs in creative writing in the United States. The first one of its kind, the Workshop was founded in 1936, and its alumni list includes some of the best known names in twentieth-century literature, including Wallace Stegner, Flannery O'Connor, Raymond Carver, and John Irving. Merely gaining admission into the program is a coveted honor for aspiring writers. Sandra Cisneros was urged by one of her college undergraduate teachers to apply to the program. When she sent in her application and writing samples, she wondered what chance a Mexican-American girl from south Chicago stood of being admitted. But, she was accepted, and in the fall of 1976 she packed up and headed to Iowa.

Not long after arriving in the university town of Iowa City, Cisneros began questioning her decision to go to graduate school. She did not fit in at the University of

Iowa and had trouble identifying with the other students. Most of them had had not spent their childhood sharing a crowded apartment with six brothers, not to mention mice and cockroaches, as Cisneros had. They had not taken countless trips back and forth between the United States and Mexico, feeling helplessly caught in the pull of these two very different cultures.

Then, Cisneros had a life-changing realization, an epiphany. She discovered a positive way to deal with her feelings of isolation and difference. Because she had lived in poverty, because she had lived a split life as both an American and a Mexican, she knew things her classmates did not. She was an expert in her own life and only she could relay the details of that life. So she began to write "about third-floor flats, and fear of rats, and drunk husbands . . . sending rocks through windows." Not only could she express her own life, she could represent her people, use her voice to echo their voices. Her readers would learn about Chicano culture and of the lives of those who lived in the exciting, complex, and sometimes difficult place between two cultures.

The short stories Cisneros began writing in Iowa were filled with the voices of her past. Eventually these stories would evolve into her first and most famous book, *The House on Mango Street.* As a child, Sandra had dreamed of being a success, of leaving her life in the Chicago tenements far behind. As a young woman, revisiting her past through her writing would bring her that success. She had to go back in order to move forward.

Sandra Cisneros was born in Chicago, Illinois, on

Chicago, the city where Sandra Cisneros was born. *(Photograph by David Head, Jr., © 2005.)*

December 20, 1954, to parents of Mexican descent. Her father, Alfredo Cisneros del Moral, had been born into a once-wealthy Mexican family with strong political connections. The family told the story of a great-grandfather who had played piano for the president of Mexico. Sandra later discovered that the family had gambled most of its money away.

As a young man in the 1940s, Alfredo enrolled in college in Mexico. His father was a strong-willed career-military man who wanted his son to be a success. But Alfredo enjoyed girls and parties more than books and classrooms, and he failed his courses. Alfredo knew he had disappointed his father and thought of running away to the United States. His father had spent time in Philadelphia, Pennsylvania and had told him stories of what the northern country was like. Afraid to face his strict father with the news of his academic failure, Alfredo illegally crossed the United States border.

When Alfredo was caught as an illegal alien, authorities gave him a choice: go back to Mexico, or join the U.S. Army and go to war. He must have truly feared his father because he chose to become a soldier and fight for the United States in World War II. While in the army, Alfredo learned only a little English. He returned to the United States after the war and decided to move to California because he knew there was a large Mexican population there. Traveling west with his brother by bus, Alfredo was unsure whether they should sit in the back or the front. In many parts of the country, forced segregation of African Americans from whites remained in effect. The brothers wondered whether their own brown skin meant they should ride in the back of the bus with the African Americans. When the bus made a stop in Chicago, Alfredo decided to get off and visit the big city for a while. It was not long before he met his future wife, Elvira Cordero Anguiano, and he decided to stay.

Sandra Cisneros knows little about her mother's family. She does not even know the name of the town in the Mexican state of Guanajuato where her maternal family lived. She describes the maternal side of her family as "simple and much more humble" than the Cisneros side, but "in many ways more admirable." Elvira's father had moved from Mexico to Chicago to work on the railroad during the Mexican revolution of 1910, to escape the violence. As soon as he had earned enough money, he brought his family north to live with him.

After marrying, Alfredo and Elvira moved into one of Chicago's poorest neighborhoods. Alfredo worked upholstering furniture and Elvira had a job in a factory, and neither of them made much money. Eventually, the couple had eight children, but only seven of them survived. Their second daughter, the next to be born after Sandra, died soon after childbirth, so Sandra grew up the only girl among six brothers. She describes the brothers as pairing up in groups of two, leaving her on her own. Sandra often wondered whether she and her sister might have been good friends. As it was, she had to occupy herself most of the time. She once explained her choice to sit alone and write by saying, "I am the only daughter in a family of six sons . . . That explains everything."

Sandra's brothers may have ignored her, but her father's attitude toward her proved even worse. At times, Alfredo even pretended not to have a daughter. The fact that her brothers left her out might have been annoying, but her father's attitude was more hurtful. Alfredo would tell people that he had seven sons, instead of six sons and a daughter. Sandra dealt with her loneliness through reading, thanks to her mother. The family had no books of its own, but Elvira made sure one of Sandra's first possessions was a library card.

Cisneros describes Elvira as a high-school dropout who loved books and passed her love of reading on to her daughter. According to Sandra, her mother surpassed Alfredo "in intelligence and social awareness," but her culture did not believe that women should be seen or heard in public. Elvira could have grown bitter, but instead she settled her dreams on her daughter. Rather than burden Sandra with the enormous amount of house-work required to support a family of nine, Elvira allowed her daughter to have time alone. Thanks to her mother, Cisneros says, "I never had to change my little brothers' diapers, I never had to cook a meal alone, nor was I ever sent to do the laundry." Elvira made sure that little interrupted Sandra's reading and homework time.

Cisneros later viewed her mother as responsible for her success. Elvira, who sang "Puccini opera" and pre-pared "a dinner for nine with only five dollars," had not finished high school, much less been to college, but she made sure her daughter would not have to miss the opportunity for a higher education herself. Later Cisneros explained to an audience of young students that she owed her success in large part to the fact that her mother "didn't want me to inherit her sadness and her rolling pin."

Cisneros began making up stories as a young child. If told to run an errand to the grocery store, for instance, she would turn the scene into a story, vividly narrating the event in her mind: "Thus clutching the coins in her pocket, our hero was off under a sky so blue and a wind so sweet she wondered it didn't make her dizzy." She tried to glamorize days that proved very lonely with few playmates. Coupled with her imagination, her constant reading served as preparation for her own writing. Rather than playing with the best friend that she wished for but never had, Sandra communed with books and their au-thors. She said these books were like "vitamins," nour-ishing her for her later writing life.

Every year, the Cisneros family would travel from Chicago to distant Mexico to visit family. *("Luminous Morning, Valley of Mexico" by Gerardo Murillo Cornadó.)*

One reason Cisneros had few friends was that her family moved fairly often, and these frequent moves were due in part to the annual journeys they made from Chicago to Mexico for extended visits with Alfredo's family. Cisneros later wrote of her father's mother that she was a spoiled woman who made no secret of the fact that Alfredo was her favorite child. This was the reason Sandra's family "returned like the tides" to Mexico every year. Each time they returned to Chicago, Sandra found herself in a new apartment building with new neighbors. No matter how many times they moved, though, every apartment was just as crowded as the last. As Cisneros later wrote, the children slept "on the living room couch and fold-out Lazy Boy, and on beds set up in the middle room, where the only place with any privacy was the bathroom."

Accompanying the moves from apartment to apartment, Cisneros also moved in and out of various Catholic schools. Not only did she not make friends at the new schools, she felt disrupted by the travel between cultures.

In Mexico, she was not accepted as Mexican, but in the United States, she did not fit in as a typical American either.

The Cisneros family lived in a part of town populated by immigrants from many Spanish-speaking countries and second-generation Americans. Residents called their neighborhood by its Spanish name, the *barrio*. Most Anglos (whites) did not know how to refer to the Spanish-speaking people who lived there. Some labeled them all Hispanic, but that term did not distinguish between their various ethnic backgrounds. Many in the *barrio* came from Mexico and Puerto Rico, and they wanted a label that would indicate those different countries of origin. The Cisneros family referred to themselves as Latinos, for the males, and Latinas, for the females. This term indicates a background in either Central or South America. Sandra Cisneros, though, prefers the terms Chicano and Chicana because they refer specifically to Mexican Americans.

While negotiating the differences between her two cultures was often difficult, Sandra later described feeling lucky to have grown up in a bilingual family. "I grew up with a Chicana mother and a Mexican father, and we spoke English to her and Spanish to him." She would not fully appreciate the value of knowing both English and Spanish until she was an adult, however. During one lecture, she stated that her mother supplied "the fierce language," while her father "gave her the language of tenderness (*'quien me dio el lenguaje de la ternura'*)." She provided the following examples. Her mother might

The Cisneros family lived in a Chicago neighborhood filled with other Spanish-speaking residents. *(Photograph by David Head, Jr., © 2005.)*

say, "Good lucky I raised you kids right so you wouldn't hang around with the punks and floozies on the corner," while her father would say things like, "Eat a little bit more, my heaven, before leaving the table and fill your tum-tum up good."

Like many children, Cisneros could lose herself in her imagination. She wrote her first poem at age ten, but, for the most part, she did not share her writing. The things she recorded in her spiral notebook remained private. As she later pointed out, "When did I talk to anyone and when did anyone ever talk to me?" Her parents cautioned her against playing with barrio children, kids they called "that kind." They told her not to behave like "*gente baja*," people from the lower class that she saw everywhere around her.

Sandra sometimes escaped her isolation by reading fairy tales. One of her favorites was "Six Swans," a Hans Christian Andersen story about one girl with many brothers, just like Sandra. The sister rescues her brothers from a spell that has turned them into swans. Sandra not only identified with the girl, she also identified with the role of caring for swans, especially, perhaps, because the name Cisneros means "keeper of swans." She also loved realistic stories with a fairy-tale quality. Stories like those written by Horatio Alger that told of very poor young men gaining power and wealth helped keep her dream of a better future alive.

For a long time, however, that better future would remain a distant and unrealized dream. Cisneros later remembered a time when believing in dreams caused her to be disappointed. In 1966, at age eleven, she learned that her family would at last move into an actual house; no more apartments or crowded tenements. She imagined a luxurious house with all the room a girl could want. But when her family arrived at the new house, it looked nothing like the one she had imagined. Instead, it was small and crooked, cramped and old. She soon came to appreciate the move into the Chicago neighborhood known as Humboldt Park. Even if she did not care for the house, the neighborhood became her home. At last Cisneros had a permanent place, a place where faces and names would become familiar parts of her life.

In this neighborhood, Cisneros began to understand

the pressures she faced in trying to adapt to dual cultures, Chicano and American. She would later refer to the experience of "straddling these two cultures" as a "balancing act" in which she tried to "define some middle ground." Some members of the Chicano culture called people like Cisneros traitors for trying to adapt to America. At the same time, she never felt accepted as an American either. For some Chicanos, particularly women, attempts to live such a split life led to depression, even thoughts of suicide. Cisneros eventually managed to handle her feelings of being rejected by both cultures by writing. Through her writing she could define what she wanted for herself, rather than what her split cultures seemed to demand.

But all of this would come much later. Still trying to find her place in the two worlds, Sandra began as a young girl to observe the people around her. Although she did not know it then, she was already beginning to collect the stories that would later become a part of *The House on Mango Street*. The Cisneros family's move into their own house, however imperfect that house may have been, represented a crucial step in Sandra's becoming a writer. Sandra Cisneros would eventually escape from her impoverished Chicago childhood and her feelings of isolation, but not without great effort.

Chapter Two

From Duckling to Swan

Sandra Cisneros did not particularly enjoy grade school. Later, when she became a well-known author, she would often visit grade schools to speak to the children. Of one of these schools, she later wrote, "the buildings smelled exactly the same as every grade school I'd ever attended, like chalk and floor wax." She went on to compare herself to "a Pavlovian puppy," meaning that she resembled a dog trained by a famous Russian scientist named Ivan Petrovich Pavlov. In his study, Pavlov would ring a bell before feeding the dog. Before long, the dog would begin to drool whenever it heard the bell, even when no food followed. The dog became conditioned, or trained, to react in a certain way whenever it heard the sound of the bell. Like the puppy reacting to the bell, the grown-up Sandra wrote that the scent of the grade school "filled my belly with fear." Her early negative experiences in school conditioned her to dislike even the buildings themselves.

As a child, Sandra attended several schools that she thought looked like prisons, "big, hulky, and authoritarian, the kind of architecture meant to instill terror." She filled her days with reading and studying at home instead of interacting with her classmates. The Cisneros family owned only two books, a Bible and an old copy of *Alice*

St. Callistus, one of the Catholic schools where Sandra attended elementary school. *(Photograph by David Head, Jr., © 2005.)*

in Wonderland. Luckily for her, there was a school library, and the school required students to use it. No one had to force Sandra to comply. She did not discover for several years that people could actually buy books from a store and bring them home to keep. From the beginning, Sandra envisioned books as things so valuable that a special building, a library, had to house them.

With her library card, Sandra possessed a key to another world. She read obsessively, sometimes even rereading the same book again and again. The book that she reread most often, Virginia Lee Burton's *The Little House,* featured one of Sandra's favorite topics: a well-loved house. She cherished that library book so much that she considered stealing it, but her Catholic training would not allow her to go through with the plan.

In the book, a little house, proud and alone in a country setting, shelters a loving family. It gazes up at the stars at night, happily watching the seasons change, and longs to know more about the city, whose distant lights it can see. Eventually, the city grows larger and larger until it surrounds the little house. Soon busy streets filled with noisy traffic replace the once quiet, rural setting. The family moves away, abandoning the house they had so loved. City lights block the house's view of the stars, and it falls into disrepair. Just when the situation seems hopeless, the great-granddaughter of the man who built the little house returns to save it. The house is loaded aboard a truck and taken back to the countryside where it can once again be happy. The story conveys a love of place and the possibility of changing one's circumstances.

Thanks to her mother, Sandra had a quiet place in her crowded house where she could read without distraction. Elvira Cisneros continued to raise Sandra differently from other Mexican-American girls, and it was to Sandra's benefit that Elvira rejected the role model of her own mother, who had lived in the kitchen and only served others. Elvira also protected her daughter from interruptions. If Sandra wanted to write poetry or work on a paper and her brothers were bothering her, Sandra would yell, "Mom! The kids are in here!" Elvira would command the boys to leave Sandra alone.

Sandra grew up believing that she had the right to her own space. She often irritated her brothers by demanding that they turn off the television to give her the quiet she needed in order to study, explaining that she could not write with noise in the background or with anyone standing close by. Slowly she began to turn her loneliness into something positive, a time in which she could read, think, and create.

When she was a teenager, Sandra began to write more seriously. In 1968, she entered Josephinum High School. She viewed herself as an ugly duckling and hoped she might be a late bloomer like some of the story characters she had grown up reading about. Although she felt ready to begin relationships with boys, few of them seemed interested in her. She later told an interviewer that this was probably a good thing, as she would have thrown herself "into love the way some warriors throw themselves into fighting." Because no one in her family or religious community discussed sex with her, she might

Cisneros attended Josephinum Catholic High School. *(Photograph by David Head, Jr., © 2005.)*

easily have become pregnant, confusing sex for love. Luckily for Cisneros, who "was ready to sacrifice everything in the name of love," no boys even asked her out, much less asked her for sex.

Even though Sandra was not part of the popular dating crowd, her fellow students began to listen to her poetry. By the time she reached her senior year, Sandra was an editor of the school's creative writing journal and considered by her classmates to be the school's resident poet. When she was not writing on paper, Sandra was composing stories and poems in her head. She learned to be a collector of facts, names, people, and events, some of which later turned up in her writing.

One of Sandra's high school teachers wrote poetry,

and she encouraged her students to do creative writing of their own. As a beginning writer, Sandra based her own poetry on topics of the day, some serious, and some not. She later described her poems as "filled . . . with pleas for peace and saving the environment," adding that, "here and there I threw in a few catchy words like ecology and Coca-Cola." While she enjoyed playing around with sounds and words, she had yet to discover her own distinct voice.

When Cisneros decided to attend college, she was afraid her family might laugh at her. Her brothers did make fun of the idea, but Alfredo Cisneros surprised her by seeming pleased. Only later did she realize that he thought college was a place for a young woman to find a husband. Although he did not offer the type of encouragement that Cisneros needed, he did not discourage her either. Because he felt his daughter would be at college mainly to find someone to marry and not to receive an education, he did not care which subject she chose as her major. That gave Cisneros the freedom to study whatever she wanted. Her choice to major in English, a topic that might have seemed impractical to some, did not bother Alfredo.

Following high school graduation in 1972, Cisneros enrolled on scholarship in a Jesuit college in Chicago, Loyola University. (Jesuits are a religious order of the Roman Catholic Church.) From the beginning, she could be distinguished from other students by her dark skin. As one of the few Chicanas on campus, Cisneros attracted attention. The students accepted her, however, and she

Cisneros attended undergraduate school at Loyola University, a Catholic school in Chicago. *(Photograph by David Head, Jr., © 2005.)*

liked college much more than she had high school. She threw herself into the study of literature. Like most students of literature, Cisneros found that the close reading of so many well-wrought works helped her own writing tremendously. One thing she noticed right away, however, were the limits of what her instructors called "the canon." The canon was made up of all the literature considered to be classic and worthy of study by college students. Most of the authors in the canon were white males. One exception was Emily Dickinson, Cisneros's favorite American poet.

Cisneros enrolled in a creative writing workshop in 1974, her third year at Loyola. The workshop required students to write poetry or fiction and then exchange their writing with others in the group. In a peer review, each student commented on the work of his or her fellow students. The workshop taught Cisneros to examine her own work more objectively, to come back to each draft again and again, looking for ways to improve it. For the first time she really listened to her own words as she read her work aloud. She also looked to new models for her poetry. One of those models, poet Donald Justice, taught at the University of Iowa.

The University of Iowa was the first school in America to establish a program exclusively dedicated to the study and practice of creative writing. Known informally as the Iowa Writers' Workshop, the program has produced a wealth of fiction writers and poets since its founding in 1936. Today, countless universities offer graduate degrees in creative writing, in programs modeled loosely on Iowa's. Still, the original maintains its reputation as one of the best and most prestigious among the many. When Cisneros's creative writing instructor at Loyola suggested that she apply to graduate school there, Sandra hesitated. What chance did she have to be accepted? And if she was accepted, was she sure she wanted to go on to more years of university?

During her senior year, Cisneros decided to apply to Iowa after all. To do so, she had to submit copies of her best writing. When Cisneros learned that she had been accepted to the Iowa Writers' Workshop for the fall semester of 1976 she could hardly believe it. She would be able to study with the great Donald Justice. Although nervous about leaving Chicago, Cisneros felt her self-confidence rise. She barely had time to enjoy being a college graduate before leaving for Iowa.

Studying writing at Iowa turned out to be a different experience from the one Sandra had anticipated. She did not get to spend the year studying with Justice, as he left the school just months after her arrival to work on his own writing. Worse than his departure, though, was the return of that familiar feeling of isolation. To Cisneros, most of the students seemed to come from more sophisticated and privileged backgrounds than her own. She was uncomfortable trying to relate to them because she shared little of their experiences. They, in turn, had no way of relating to the struggle to survive in one tenement apartment after another. Sandra asked herself, "What could I know? My classmates were from the best schools in the country." She labored to get beyond her uncertainty and find value in her own experiences.

In "Boys & Girls," one of the vignettes that make up *The House on Mango Street,* the main character thinks of herself as "a balloon tied to an anchor." That description could very well have applied to Cisneros in graduate school. She had moved to Iowa with the hope of developing her talent so she could fly above her feelings of inadequacy. Instead, they stayed with her and threatened to drag her into failure. Further increasing Cisneros's feeling of isolation was the intense competition among the students. Each wrote under enormous pressure as they tried to produce the best work in the group.

Even the way writing was approached in her classes did not seem to apply to Cisneros. In one meeting, the class discussed an author's symbolic use of houses. That author, Gaston Bachelard, used houses to represent the inner lives of humans. The students viewed a house as representing their sense of self-identity, even their imagination. Cisneros found it unsettling to think of her crooked old house representing her soul. The house her family had finally been able to afford was an ugly little bungalow in one of Chicago's poor Puerto Rican neighborhoods, and Sandra had hated it. How could she consider that house as something that stood for her hopes and dreams? She wondered if she were the only one in her class who felt she did not fit in.

As she worked at her writing, Cisneros tried to ignore her feelings of isolation. She learned to perfect her talent for listening to the voices around her and recalling the voices in her memory. She wrote poems that were little more than monologues (a speech given by a character to no one in particular). She incorporated the Iowa voices that she was hearing for the first time, the sound of the

Midwest farmers. She also began to use voices from her past, voices from the barrio. These voices from her Chicano culture would one day become her focus.

Cisneros at last came to realize that she had a distinctive voice of her own. The realization seemed to come to her suddenly, as she later explained: "It was not until this moment when I separated myself, when I considered myself truly distinct, that my writing acquired a voice . . . I knew I was a Mexican woman. But, I didn't think it had anything to do with why I felt so much imbalance in my life, whereas it had everything to do with it!" She would soon learn that writing required a special power, and her unique power was her connection to two different cultures. The differences that had in the past seemed a weakness, the cause of her isolation and dissatisfaction, now became her strength. "This is how *The House on Mango Street* was born, the child-voice that was to speak all my poems for many years," Cisneros later wrote of her realization.

At Iowa, Cisneros began writing the kinds of stories and poems that she had always wanted to read as a young person. Her poetry told of poverty and hunger, but also of hope, symbolized, for instance, by beautiful flowers that grew among the stone buildings. As well, her poems were filled with characters similar to herself, and carried titles like "Earl of Tennessee," "Louis, His Cousin and His Other Cousin," and "Edna's Ruthie." She sometimes even set her poems directly in the barrio, such as when she returns to a neighborhood furniture store in her poem "Gil's Furniture Bought & Sold."

Eventually, Cisneros did make friends in the Iowa program. One of them, Joy Harjo, was a Creek Indian from Oklahoma. She, too, knew of a life separate and apart from the white majority. While Cisneros had matured in the barrio, Harjo had grown up on an American Indian reservation. Harjo would later become famous for her poetry and her music, but for the time being, the two young women encouraged one another as beginning writers. Another close friend from Iowa was the fiction writer Dennis Mathis. Mathis would later become Cisneros's editor as she assembled her stories into *The House on Mango Street*. Cisneros also searched for support and encouragement in literature written by others who were not from the mainstream, Anglo culture, reading works by Chinese-American writer Maxine Hong Kingston and Toni Morrison, an African American.

When Cisneros discovered her own voice, she began to reconsider what she had previously believed about literature and those who wrote it. In many instances, simply having talent was not enough; one also needed encouragement and resources. Cisneros was fortunate enough to have received scholarships to schools that allowed her to learn from other writers and develop her own talent. The characters that filled her stories, though, were from the poor and working classes, and few of them could have afforded the luxury of time to write.

Cisneros recalled that even her beloved Emily Dickinson (1838-1886) had employed an Irish housekeeper, who likely did many of Dickinson's household chores. Dickinson herself had an education, something many women of that time lacked. She had her own room in a home she shared with her sister and money she had inherited from her father. These facts contributed toward her success as a writer, if only because they provided her with the time, space, and security to focus on her writing. She did not have to worry about supporting herself through writing; her incredible collection of 1,775 poems did not even see publication until after her death. But Dickinson's servant did not have the same privileges her employer had. Cisneros wondered "if Emily Dickinson's Irish housekeeper wrote poetry or if she ever had the secret desire to study and be anything besides a housekeeper." Cisneros saw the maid as a similar figure to her own mother, who had sacrificed in order that Sandra could pursue her art.

Women overcoming their traditional roles would become a major theme in Cisneros's work over the years. She wanted to free those women from knowing themselves only through their service to others. When she looked around, Cisneros saw women who served husbands as wives, children as mothers, and fathers as daughters, leaving precious little energy and time for themselves. In addition, the women from Cisneros's culture had to struggle to adapt to a new American culture, while also functioning in a Latino community. The demands proved overwhelming at times. Not many minutes in a typical day could be devoted to the creative pursuits that Cisneros believed would help each woman discover her individual identity. Cisneros would serve her community by featuring these women's stories, opening their lives up to outsiders who knew little about the barrio or the people who lived there.

Cisneros left her ugly-duckling image far behind as she matured through her writing into the promise of the swan. Now she had to claim that promise and fulfill her destiny as a writer. She also had to support herself, though, and time spent working would be time taken away from her writing. The need for a steady income threatened to derail her writing career. She had little choice, however, but to work. Ten long years would pass before she could finally declare herself free of that need and devote all her time to her writing. In the meantime, she would do everything she could to make her writing possible.

Chapter Three

Like Pearls on a Necklace

In 1978, Sandra Cisneros graduated from Iowa with a master of fine arts degree in creative writing. Although she had begun writing the sketches that would make up her first book, she was not yet prepared to write full time. She returned to Chicago and became a school counselor.

Cisneros later remarked that, even though she held a master's degree, she never thought of applying to teach at a college or university because she did not think of herself as qualified. Like many women of minority background, she had never been encouraged to believe she had anything to offer. Even with the completion of a master's degree, she did not yet have the confidence to apply for such a job.

At the Latino Youth Alternative High School she faced the great challenge of working with high school dropouts whose experience of childhood had been anything but status quo. After two years of learning about "meter and metaphor" at the now far-distant Writers' Workshop,

Cisneros was suddenly faced with teaching students who had survived all sorts of horrors. They told her about seeing people they knew involved in drive-by shootings, witnessing violent robberies, and surviving when their run-down apartment buildings caught fire. These were not experiences teenagers should have to deal with. Some had been unable to cope with the stress of an abusive family life, and they had joined the homeless on the streets rather than stand by while their fathers abused their mothers. Some, instead of running away, "drank and drugged themselves" or "mothered three kids before they were eighteen." Cisneros found herself back in the barrio, living, through her students, the stories she had begun writing.

Cisneros began to share her work with others by giving public readings, and soon her writing was well known in the local community. Those in the local community came to know her work. The Chicago Transit Authority (CTA), which manages the city's public transportation, began a poetry project with the help of the Poetry Society of America, and Cisneros was among the featured poets. The CTA collected poems from across the country to post inside buses and train cars. Cisneros's work joined that of famous poets, including Chicago's Gwendolyn Brooks and Illinois poet Carl Sandburg. Every day hundreds of people read the poetry as they commuted to and from work; they may not have known Cisneros's face, but they came to know her words.

While working at the alternative school, Cisneros absorbed material for her poems and stories by listening to her students. She not only listened to what they said, but to how they said it. She later wrote that her students may not have been accomplished writers, but "man, could they talk a good story." When she compared their accomplishments to her own education, she realized that they "held doctorates from the university of life." Cisneros wanted to let the students know that their "lives were extraordinary, that they were extraordinary for having survived." She would eventually do this through *The House on Mango Street.*

Through the CTA poetry project and her readings, Sandra's writing gained the attention of other writers. Mexican American Gary Soto was one of the writers who recognized Cisneros as an up-and-coming talent. With his help, in 1980 she published her first book, a small collection of poetry commonly known as a chapbook. She called the collection *Bad Boys.* In the poems, Cisneros's voice rang strong, painting a picture of her Chicago barrio. Printed by a small group, Mango Press of San Jose, California, *Bad Boys* delighted its small audience. Less than 1,000 copies were printed, and it remained hard to find in later years. Fortunately for her fans, Cisneros later included the poems in her third book, *My Wicked Wicked Ways,* which would be published in 1987.

As Cisneros read her poetry at Chicago coffeehouses and schools, she was flattered by the attention her writing received. However, she worried about the fact that she did not have enough time to perfect her craft. Her work with students enriched her life in ways she could not have anticipated. She recognized herself in the many young faces that she saw during assemblies. Later she would write of the girls who heard her speak, that they were "too timid to raise their hand and ask me a question, too shy to even make eye contact." She went on, talking of how they would "laugh behind cupped hands and hunker themselves between hunched shoulders as if they could make themselves disappear." Once, she had been that girl who wanted to disappear. Now that she could express those feelings she had repressed, she had to find the time and energy to do so.

In 1980, Cisneros decided to leave the Alternative High School and return to Loyola University, the school that had awarded her undergraduate degree, this time as an employee. There, she worked in administration as an assistant who recruited high school students to enroll at Loyola. She went into the barrios where prospective students could feel comfortable talking and listening to a fellow Chicana. She understood, though, that many of the students she spoke with would never attend college. They lacked not only the resources but the necessary support from their families as well. This remained especially true for the young women. Caught up in the traditions of Mexican culture, many of them accepted a future of marriage and motherhood.

As for her own romantic life, Cisneros dated and had steady boyfriends from time to time. However, she never seriously considered marriage, for fear that she would no longer be able to work. Her first serious boyfriend, an Anglo, pressured her to marry, to set as her goal a "house in the suburbs." He did not realize that she needed her time alone to shape her art. More importantly, not sharing Cisneros's background, he did not understand her need to accomplish something great for her own people. She knew this was because "he wasn't Mexican, didn't grow up poor, and had no ambition to be/do anything in his life other than buy that house, put his feet up and sigh."

As part of her continuing attempt to resolve her two cultures, Cisneros wrote in a combination of English and Spanish. She retains a spattering of Spanish words in her poetry and fiction and rarely translates the Spanish words for her English-speaking readers. The translations would interrupt the flow of her stories, she has said, and leave "the seams showing."

In the early 1980s, she wrote the stories "Alicia Who Sees Mice," "Sally," and "What Sally Said," among others. She began to envision her stories as an interconnected collection. Each one related to the other, yet each could also be read and understood on its own. The pattern took shape and became the novel *The House on Mango Street*. Putting that book together, Cisneros discovered, would require her complete concentration. But turning her full attention to her art still seemed beyond her reach. She still lacked the crucial resources of time, money, and confidence.

Then, in 1982, a temporary solution to Cisneros's problems arrived in the form of a grant awarded to Cisneros by the National Endowment for the Arts (NEA). This sum of money would allow her to quit work and focus solely on her writing. In addition, Nick Kanellos, publisher of the small Arte Público Press, encouraged her to devote herself full time to writing. Kanellos had edited one of Cisneros's short stories, and he recognized her talent immediately. The encouragement he gave her was exactly what she needed during this period of insecurity. She accepted his guidance and arranged for his press to publish her first book of fiction.

Cisneros had to finish some literary projects to which she had already committed herself and work another six months at her job. After completing those obligations she moved, in 1981, to Provincetown, Massachusetts. She was both physically and mentally escaping Chicago and the barrio. She chose Provincetown in order to be close to Dennis Mathis, a man Cisneros called her "best buddy from Iowa days." Also a fic-

Cisneros at times felt trapped by the need to make a living. *(Photograph by David Head, Jr., ©2005.)*

tion writer, Mathis agreed to help his old friend shape her book.

Cisneros felt fortunate to have Mathis's help. She later wrote, "He was my editor for what I feel are the cleanest pieces in the book." Those pieces include the chapters from *Mango Street* called "My Name," "Hips," and "Elenita, Cards, Palm, Water." Cisneros assembled her stories like a series of pearls on a necklace. While each "pearl" could be appreciated for its individual beauty, it could also be appreciated for its connection to the stories that preceded and followed. Cisneros eventually strung together forty-four different vignettes, or little stories, that ranged from one-and-a-half pages to three pages in length. Under contract to Arte Público Press, she worked hard to complete the collection.

It seems possible that Cisneros fashioned the narrator of *The House on Mango Street,* a young girl named Esperanza Cordero, on herself. From the book's first sentence, Cisneros's own story rings forth: "We didn't always live on Mango Street." Esperanza lists the several places the family had lived, saying that she cannot even remember them all. Then she adds, "But what I remember most is moving a lot." While Cisneros's last name has an important meaning, keeper of the swans, Esperanza's first name is also highly symbolic; it means "hope." And, as Cisneros had done as a child, in *The House on Mango Street,* Esperanza hopes for a house, a real home for her family of six.

When Esperanza moves onto Mango Street, she feels ashamed of her house and its run-down condition. That house comes to represent her poverty and the shame she occasionally feels for being poor. She does not want to admit that she lives there. Esperanza is determined to move into a house of her own someday, and talks of wanting "only a house quiet as snow, a space for myself to go, clean as the paper before the poem." In fiction, the inside of a house has often represented the "proper" place for a woman. For Cisneros, and for Esperanza, it comes to represent a space in which to create her art. Esperanza realizes that she wants to be a writer. In the book's twenty-fourth vignette, "Born Bad," Esperanza shares a secret with her aunt. That secret is that she writes poetry.

Over the course of the novel, Esperanza matures both physically and emotionally. In literary terms, the stories represented a *bildungsroman,* or a story about a child growing up. Typically, if the child was male, he gained some type of treasure at the story's end, usually his independence as an adult. The young boy had to endure several trials, and by surviving, he proved himself worthy of that freedom. If a bildungsroman featured a young girl, she generally passed her trials in order to learn proper behavior. Esperanza broke that pattern, surviving her trials with the help of her writing, and gaining independence from the barrio through her creativity.

The *Mango Street* vignettes read like poetry. Cisneros fills them with sharp images, sounds, and metaphors. Cisneros has called the stories "lazy poems," meaning that each vignette could have been developed into a poem, but that their messages seem stronger in story form. While Cisneros filled the book with hope, as Esperanza's name emphasizes, she also confronted the problems of the barrio in an honest manner.

Some people would later remark that what Cisneros wrote could be problematic, that readers would only see a young woman trapped by her culture and her poverty. But Cisneros explained that the story needed this realism to counteract dangerous images of the barrio regularly presented on television and in the media. By dangerous she referred not to violence but rather to falsehoods. These images were too often lies, depicting a "Sesame Street" picture of a place "warm and beautiful." She wrote that a poor neighborhood may seem charming at first glance, but those who must live there see it differently. They have to deal with the piles of garbage left in the streets, shootings of children, the ever-present rats, and the dilapidated housing.

The House on Mango Street is a work of fiction, though, and does not reproduce or even necessarily represent Cisneros's own life. Rather, while the stories are loosely derived from experiences she or her students may have had, these experiences have been shaped into works of fiction, with many details changed, rearranged, made up, and omitted. Cisneros later commented that students question her about whether or not her stories are true. She explains that all fiction has basis in truth. While she does not write autobiography, the true or exact story of her life, all of her stories are "lived, or witnessed, or heard: stories that were told to me." With these stories, Cisneros gave voice to the little girl from the barrio, and to the girl's wide array of friends, family, and neighbors.

Cisneros would later write that, until the Iowa Writers' Workshop, she had not thought of her home or the members of her family or neighborhood worth writing about. To her, they did not seem unusual or unique. She was so accustomed to the daily goings on in her neighborhood, the way people talked and passed their time, the way her own family lived, that she could not see what was special about it right away. Because her family did not resemble those on popular television sitcoms, she did not see them as worthy topics for her writing. Once she moved past that attitude and decided that she could not imitate mainstream culture or the common subjects and styles of fiction, Esperanza took shape in her mind.

Ultimately, Esperanza triumphs over her poverty. She leaves the barrio. Cisneros left her barrio too, but she has never abandoned the place or its people. About leaving she later wrote, "It's a circular thing, you leave, but you also do other work to enable other people to control their destinies."

Still, Cisneros did not feel in total control of her own destiny. The deadline by which she had to have her manuscript complete was fast approaching, and Sandra worried about not meeting it. She needed to take control.

Chapter Four

Crossing Borders

As the first deadline for handing the manuscript over to Arte Público Press approached, Cisneros asked Kanellos for more time. Concerned over her inability to meet the deadline, she decided a change of surroundings might help her writing. She still had money left over from her NEA grant. She decided to go to Europe. The very day the manuscript had been scheduled for completion, Cisneros left for Greece.

At 4 AM on the day of her second deadline, November 30, 1982, Cisneros at last completed the book. She had been mailing individual pieces to Kanellos as she finished them. Once Kanellos reviewed her manuscript, she would still need to do some revising. Restless and still lacking focus, Cisneros decided on another change of scenery and moved to France. The editor at Público Press encouraged her to continue to revise, telling her he did not feel the manuscript was "quite there." She agreed with him and spent the next two years rewriting it.

During that time, Cisneros continued to mature as both a writer and a person. She completed the revisions in 1984, and "that was that."

Waiting for the book to appear later that year made Cisneros nervous. Like most writers, she worried about how reviewers would comment on her work. She had grown used to focusing on one story at a time, and found it difficult to think of the book as a whole. She wondered whether she had even written what she had set out to write. Two days after finishing the book, she wrote to a friend about "the terror of having to live with *Mango Street*." Stitching her stories together had seemed like "making a quilt by the light of a flashlight." Now, as its creator, she would have to accept it, whether it was perfect or not.

Cisneros spent the spring of 1983 in Venice, Italy, during which time she served as artist-in-residence at the Michael Karolyi Foundation. (Artists-in-residence generally visit an institution or school for a set length of time, teaching, giving lectures, and working at their art.) In that position, she taught a few hours each week while having her living expenses paid for by the host institution. Cisneros worked to add additional poems to a collection that she envisioned as a book titled *My Wicked Wicked Ways*.

Traveling around Europe allowed Cisneros to continually learn about other countries and their inhabitants. While their cultures may have differed somewhat from her own, she found she could identify with individuals, regardless of their nationalities. One of those individuals was a Yugoslav woman named Jasna K., with whom she would form a life-long friendship. She met Jasna during the summer of 1983, when she moved to Yugoslavia to stay with a man she had met. She later remembered those weeks in Yugoslavia as a time of playing wife. In charge of the household, she struggled to find basics, such as toilet paper, in the Communist country. She spent many hours cleaning and gardening, duties that contrasted strongly with her writing.

Cisneros met Jasna for the first time in the garden they shared. Although they knew nothing about one another, she felt a *simpatico,* a sympathy and friendliness, for Jasna. The two became close friends, sharing household items along with stories. Before long, Cisneros felt she had known Jasna forever. A divorcée, Jasna lived with her mother. Jasna would later help to translate some of Cisneros's writing into her own language of Serbo-Croatian.

Cisneros forged many close friendships with European women in a relatively short time. It seemed she had discovered a community of women with whom she shared a great deal. She said of these relationships, "women helped me and they asked for nothing in return, and they gave me great compassion and love when I was feeling lost and alone." Their basic concerns for respect, love, and dignity did not vary, regardless of their ethnic backgrounds. While she had always appreciated women and the hard work their roles demanded, this appreciation grew when she discovered the many similarities between women of different cultures. Like Cisneros, many struggled to find a means of support as they attempted to pursue their art.

Cisneros's experiences during her European travels helped strengthen her resolve to be a spokesperson for all struggling people, particularly women. She would later choose to reject marriage and the role of serving a family in order to devote all her time and energy to her writing. Not only would she use her writing to highlight issues such as poverty and education, she would become a public activist.

Cisneros returned to the United States in 1984 in order to be present for the publication of *The House on Mango Street*. She continued to write poetry for a few months as she awaited the reviews. The last of the grant money she had been living on was about to run out. When the reviews at last appeared, most of them were positive. Many critics praised her work as something new—a novel by a Chicana that spoke to the concerns of her people in a way that had never been attempted. Cisneros was also praised for introducing an entirely new audience to Mexican-American culture. Through Esperanza, Cisneros showed readers that many young people share the same hopes and concerns, regardless of background or ethnic identity.

Some reviewers did not react positively to Cisneros's poetic approach to writing fiction. One *Booklist* critic wrote that her "loose and deliberately simple style," mixing poetry with prose, at times "annoys" with its "cuteness." He did not agree with others who found that her compositional style actually allowed for a deeper

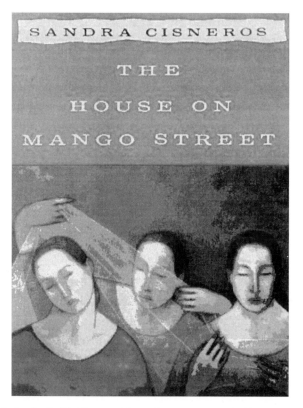

Cisneros's first book, *The House on Mango Street,* was greeted with rave reviews upon publication. *(Cover of* The House on Mango Street *reproduced courtesy of Random House, Inc.)*

exploration and understanding of the book's themes.

Cisneros once said in a speech that when she can right away find the "words to express her idea," it becomes fiction, a story. When the words are more difficult to come by, she produces poetry instead. Gary Soto found her approach to writing appealing. He called Cisneros "foremost a storyteller," regardless of the form she chose. Barbara Kingsolver (an American writer living in the southwest, whose own novels often feature Latin-American characters) explained that the choice to write fiction rather than poetry is a practical one in the United States, where poets do not receive much credit. As she puts it, "Elsewhere, poets have the cultural status of our rock stars and the income of our romance novelists. Here, a poet is something your mother probably didn't want you to grow up to be."

Publication of *The House on Mango Street* was accompanied by attention and praise for the young Chicana writer. The novel won the Before Columbus American Book Award, an award presented annually to acknowledge the excellence and diversity of American writing. However, favorable reviews and awards did not yield enough money that Cisneros could consider supporting herself solely with her writing. Once again, she began looking for a job.

In 1984, Sandra Cisneros found herself on her way to San Antonio, Texas, where she would begin a new job as the arts administrator at the Guadalupe Arts Center. In San Antonio, Cisneros discovered a community of Spanish speaking people made up of Mexican Americans, Mexicans, and people from all over Latin America. This community instantly made her feel at home. She enjoyed the barrio community in San Antonio much more than the Chicago barrio she had grown up in.

While a great many Chicanos lived in both Illinois and Texas, their attitudes were quite different in one state from the other. In Texas, people were physically closer to the border with Mexico, yet distant on an emotional

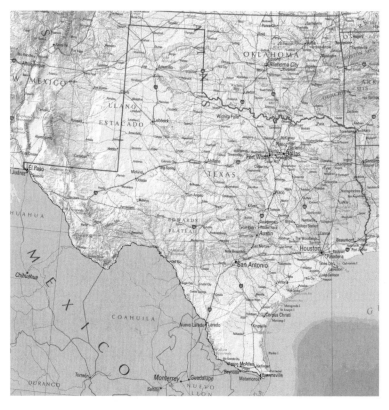

A map of the state of Texas. Texans are notoriously proud of their heritage; Cisneros would experience both the positive and the negative sides of this while living there. *(University of Texas map collection.)*

level. They felt a loyalty to Texas, in spite of the years of conflict between Texas and their homeland. Many of them had been in Texas for centuries; they were Texans, adopting the label *Tejanos*. In Chicago, people were physically farther away from Mexico, yet closer emotionally because most had not been there for more than one or two generations. As newcomers to Chicago, they

The Spanish and Mexican influence is everywhere apparent in San Antonio. Above, one of the city's numerous Spanish missions, Mission San Jose y San Miguel de Aguayo. *(Texas Highway Department.)*

remained loyal to Mexico, not to Illinois. Cisneros found that people in Texas expected her to be a snob, to feel she was superior because she was born in a midwestern state. But, she had few emotional ties to Illinois and felt an immediate sense of belonging in Texas's Chicano community. In Texas she felt, more than ever, that her choice to become a spokesperson for the Chicano community had been the right one.

In addition to working her new job, Cisneros volunteered to help to bring the arts to the local Chicano community. She also wanted the white community to recognize the rich Latino cultural heritage around them. Cisneros planned an event that brought a number of Latino writers to San Antonio to participate in a celebration of their cultures' stories. To her disappointment, not many people from outside the barrio attended. Her frustration mounted over the continuing gap between the white and brown cultures.

Cisneros later admitted to developing a racist attitude toward whites during these years. Even though she thought of herself as a feminist, she could not feel empathy for upper-class white women. Only if they appeared willing to move toward an understanding of her world and her culture could she feel compassion. She had grown up knowing of their world so they, in turn, should take an interest in hers. Previously, she had tried hard to fit into a white world. She later said that, although she had spent her life "trying to be like my women friends in school. I didn't have any white women friends when I was in Texas." That realization made her angry.

Despite these disappointments, Cisneros loved living in San Antonio. For the first time, she felt that she actually fit into a community. She felt comfortable living as a Chicana so close to the country of Mexico. In addition, San Antonio as a whole did value the arts, even the arts of Mexican Americans. Cisneros admired the amount of knowledge and pride San Antonians had where Texas history was concerned. The sense of place proved extremely attractive to Cisneros. Spanish words floated around constantly, and she gained a new appreciation for the rhythms of the language.

Even though she enjoyed her work and the people she worked with, she again found herself without enough time to write. She needed energy for her art, but her time was occupied with the need to make a living. At the end of the day, her writing was the family she came home to and nurtured. Cisneros later told one interviewer, "I had to be a teacher, a counselor, I've had to work as an Arts Administrator, you know, all kinds of things just to make my living. The writing is always what you try to save energy for, it's your child."

In 1985, help for her financial problems ar-

A sign pointing the way to the Dobie Paisano Ranch. The word paisano means roadrunner, but has other connotations besides, including "peasant," "compatriot," "native," and "rustic."

Texas folklorist and writer J. Frank Dobie built the Paisano Ranch in the Texas Hill Country outside Austin as a retreat for himself and his wife. After his death, the ranch became a retreat for writers, granting them time and space to write without concerns for worldly matters. Cisneros and her writing thrived in the secluded place.

rived in the form of another grant. Cisneros received the 1985 Dobie Paisano Fellowship, which provided her with a stipend as well as a comfortable, secluded place on a ranch outside Austin. There she could live and write in peaceful solitude for six months, concentrating solely on her poetry without having to worry about money or work. In the country, Cisneros fell deeper in love with the state of Texas. The landscape enthralled her. She wrote playfully that it seemed like a "graceful two-step, howl of an accordion, little gem and jewel," that it was both "a little sad, a little joyous" and that it "has made me whole."

Observing two cultures and two languages co-existing so well in San Antonio, Cisneros realized that, for the first time in her life, she felt as though she were home. In one memorable vignette from *Mango Street*, the character Esperanza consults a fortuneteller, seeking confirmation that she will one day have a house, a home, of her own. The fortuneteller does see a home for Espernaza, but it is "a home in the heart." In the story, Esperanza seems somewhat disappointed in this prophecy, but for Cisneros, it seems, feeling at home in Texas, at home in her heart, was not disappointing in the least.

Over the next two years, Cisneros continued her work. She began to enjoy a small amount of fame in San Antonio. People recognized her from her public readings, school presentations, and her leadership position in the arts. In 1987, *The House on Mango Street* went into its third printing, and Cisneros finished preparing a group of poems for publication. She worked hard to find a way to make a consistent living with her writing. She advertised creative writing classes, but few people responded. It was with a feeling of sorrow that she began to consider leaving the city that had at last given her a sense of place.

An opportunity for a stable income arose when California State University in Chico, California offered Cisneros a temporary position teaching creative writing. As a visiting lecturer, she would earn a fee for teaching and, presumably, still have plenty of time for her own writing. She took the job, and within a few months she was in the classroom in California.

Chapter Five

So Many Things Terrify

Cisneros was grateful for her teaching job and the income it provided. However, the demands of the classroom soon began to take a toll. Many creative writing teachers are themselves writers, and they use the time left over after class preparation, teaching, and grading to do their own work. Cisneros, though, felt guilty if she worked on her own projects. She felt she should spend all her spare time on her teaching duties.

In addition, her approach to teaching often differed from that of other teachers. Cisneros wanted to teach students to learn from their own lives, as she had done. She knew the importance of listening to the voices in one's own community; without listening, one could not write creatively. However, the university, like many institutions, focused on practical matters. When the bell signaled the end of class, the students had to pack up for their next class, whether or not the instructor had finished sharing all she had to share. To Cisneros, the fact that students had to stop writing, sometimes in mid-sentence, made no sense. At times, she wanted to continue the exchange of ideas with her students over a cup of coffee after class. The system did not welcome her approach. Once again, she struggled to find her place within a community that made demands she found difficult to meet.

Cisneros also suffered from her reputation for tardiness. Never good at meeting the demands of the clock, she often arrived late for class. Because students had to arrive on time, they felt that she did not respect them when she came in late. Cisneros felt herself torn between two worlds, the world of her art, and the world of practical demands. That conflict mirrored another, the conflict between her Mexican and American cultures. The constant pull from these various forces was frustrating and exhausting. She found the time to finish the collection of poems she had been working on , and after that, she fell into a depression.

While in Chico, Cisneros lived with the editor Norma Alarcón, a friend who encouraged her to continue her writing, regardless of the internal conflict she felt. Cisneros later recalled a nightmare from that period, in which she dreamed in Spanish. She awoke and said to herself, *"Tantas cosas asustan, tantas,"* or "So many things terrify, so many." The phrase well reflected her mood at the time, and "Tantas Cosas Asustan, Tantas" became the title of a poem written completely in Spanish. When asked why she chose the Spanish language for that poem, she explained, "When I tried to translate it into English, it sounded wrong to me and I had to leave it in Spanish." Because sound is so important in poetry, the poem would not have made sense to her in English. She could only hear the poem in Spanish.

With this choice, Cisneros experienced a small triumph over her ongoing conflict. She had chosen Spanish, the language of her ancestors, because, in this instance, it proved superior to English, the language of her native culture. The fact that she could make a clear choice between different voices for the sake of her art showed that she might overcome the conflict that had bothered her for so many years.

Cisneros had always found the voices of others fascinating, no matter where the voices came from. She said in one interview, "wherever you put me I write about what I hear." She considered herself a linguist, one who studies language, but in her case, she "was more concerned with the how than the what" contained in people's statements. In other words, she focused more on the sound and rhythms of words than on their meaning. She simply had to find a way to make the voices she heard her own. While she had made a good start with her published pieces, she did not yet feel confident that she had reached her goal.

In a speech at Indiana University in November 1986, Cisneros told her audience that she and Alarcón had discussed the subjects of their works and realized that they feature themes such as love, sex, survival, racism, and poverty. Neither woman had the "luxury . . . to write of landscapes and sunsets and tulips in a vase." Their backgrounds made them choose serious topics that related to everyday life in the cultures in which they had been raised. She added that they did not wait to be inspired, as other writers might. Instead they felt driven, even obsessed to write. Cisneros explained that if asked what exactly she wrote about, "I would have to say I write about those ghosts inside that haunt me, that will not let me sleep, of that which even memory does not like to mention." From time to time, those ghosts haunted her to the point that she felt hope slip away.

Caught in one of those periods of depression while at Chico, Cisneros lost her confidence in both her teaching and her writing. A literary agent tried to contact her about a new book contract but Cisneros would not see her. She even began to feel suicidal. At one point, she thought that dying as a young unfulfilled artist might be romantic. Later she admitted how foolish that was, but at the time, she could not seem to shake her dark emotions. Yet, she seemed to find a reason for living in her writing. She told a junior high audience at a Hispanic achievement festival in 1986, "I don't want to die young. I don't want to drive fast, or get on airplanes, or sit with my back to the door when I'm in a bar. For the sake of my writing, I want a long life."

Cisneros had to work hard at it, but she slowly emerged from this dark period. In 1987 a small publisher called Third Woman Press published the collection of poetry that she had worked on since her Iowa days, *My Wicked Wicked Ways*. Then, being awarded a second National Endowment for the Arts fellowship in fiction helped renew her confidence in herself. It also provided her with financial independence, allowing her to leave the classroom and refocus on her writing. Finally, Cisneros agreed to contact Susan Bergholz, the agent who had sought her for years.

Bergholz asked to see a few of Cisneros's new stories and within months the agent had landed a new contract for Cisneros. Random House/Vintage Press purchased the story collection, titled *Woman Hollering Creek.* Cisneros received a $100,000 "advance," a payment made to a writer before the work is completed. This amount set a record as the largest advance ever presented to a Mexican-American writer. After all her fears, Cisneros now received a financial vote of confidence from a well-respected publisher that she could not doubt. She referred to the contract as her "green card," a pass that meant she could at last stay in San Antonio without worrying about her income. She could also fulfill her desire to become a voice for her people.

In the meantime, Third Woman Press published *My Wicked Wicked Ways.* Cisneros explained that the title represented her own view of herself, and that this view was liberating. In the past, she had problems with the idea that she could construct her own future or control her fate, believing that her desire to take control would be seen as "wicked" by some. This idea perhaps grew out of her upbringing as a Catholic in the Mexican tradition. She had been taught to feel guilty about "redefining" herself or thinking of her own identity, strength, or sexuality. In one interview, she stated that as a beginning writer, she had hoped to get rid of the ghosts from her past. As she matured, she made peace with her past. Of the "ghosts," she said, "They're a part of you and you can talk about them, and I think that it's a big step to be able to say: 'Well, yeah, I'm haunted, ha!'" She liked the idea of coming to terms with her ghosts and living with them.

Cisneros played with the idea of being wicked, of being a sexual temptress, in the photograph placed on the cover of her collection. In the picture, Cisneros wears a provocatively cut dress with cowboy boots, sits cross-legged, and holds a cigarette. Red earrings and a nearby glass of red wine complement her lipsticked mouth. Although she had attempted to make fun of the idea of being wicked, some readers were made uncomfortable by the photograph. Men complained that she led them on, as she appeared to be promising a sexual experience of sorts. Some feminists expressed disapproval that Cisneros offered herself in the stereotyped image of a woman whose only importance was as a sex object.

Cisneros laughed off their objections: "I'm wearing cowboy boots! It's a fun photo." She had tried to play with the accepted idea of what a powerful woman looks like. "Why can't a feminist be sexy?" she asked, adding that her own feelings of sexiness gave her "self-empow-erment." She knew the negative reaction arose from the traditional belief that women with such self-images must be abnormal, bad, or insane. She hoped to help change these notions.

Many of the poems in the collection address ideas of wickedness, power, and sexuality. In the following excerpt from the poem that serves as the collection's preface, even her choice to pursue writing is portrayed as wicked:

> Gentlemen, ladies. If you please—these
> are my wicked poems from when.
> The girl grief decade. My wicked nun
> years, so to speak. I sinned.
>
> . . .
>
> My first felony—I took up with poetry.
>
> . . .
>
> Wife? A woman like me
> whose choice was rolling pin or factory.
> An absurd vice, this wicked wanton
> writer's life.

There is a playful tone in these lines to match the playfulness Cisneros had intended with the cover photograph.

After ten years of writing, Cisneros had attained a level of financial and personal independence. She finalized an important decision she had been wrestling with for years. She would not marry or have a family, at least not for some time. She still considered her poetry and stories to be her children, and now she finally had the time and energy to dedicate to them. In 1986, she had told a crowd of junior high students that she wanted to become one of the few authors who wrote on behalf of those lacking power. Giving as examples Emily Dickinson's housekeeper and her own mother, Cisneros claimed she wanted to express "the world of thousands of silent women" so that "their stories can finally be heard."

Although at times she considered her desire to be alone selfish, Cisneros also knew that she could only write in solitude. As a child, she had hated being friendless and alone; as an adult, she embraced the good fortune of having time and space to herself. Of course, her family-centered father, mother, and siblings did not understand her choices. One of her poems, titled "Old Maids," addresses this dilemma. In the poem, a group of unmarried women attend friends' weddings only to be questioned as to when they will marry. The questioners wonder what could have happened to the unmarried women when they were children to make them hate the idea of marriage. The voice in the poem demands that married women examine their own relationships to discover whether they are truly as happy as they think they are. Cisneros once commented in an interview that she had never known of a couple in what she would consider a "model" marriage and claimed never to have encountered a married couple who were as happy as she was living alone.

With many good friends, male and female, Cisneros was not a lonely person. Most people considered her a very social person who enjoyed good company and good conversation. However, when she wanted to be alone, they knew they had best not interrupt her. She admitted to sometimes turning her music up and dancing around the house alone in celebration of the fact that she had a house of her own with no one to look after but herself.

One interviewer commented that at the end of *My*

Wicked Wicked Ways, Cisneros still did not appear to have claimed her emotional house. Cisneros agreed, explaining that those poems had been written over a ten-year period, from her time in the Iowa workshop until just before publication. She labeled that time her "wanderings in the desert" and said that she hoped her new book of stories would at last celebrate her settling into her self, into her "new house." By this point, Cisneros seemed near the end of her conflict-filled days. Instead of allowing her emotions to rob her of her creativity, she used them to replenish her poetry and fiction.

Cisneros approached writing fiction differently than writing poetry. She described a "terrifying center" that she pursued in her poetry. She did not think about her readers, or herself, as she composed her lines. Writing poetry was like an act of discovery for Cisneros; sometimes she would come to a realization she had never considered before she started. She once stated in an interview that "When you think: 'Oh my goodness, I didn't know I felt that!' that's where you stop. That's the little piece of gold." On the other hand, when writing fiction, she knew ahead of time what she wanted to write and where the story would go. For her, a story has to be "something someone wants to listen to," so she always considers her audience when writing fiction.

Cisneros increasingly valued her solitude while working to complete *Woman Hollering Creek.* The large advance she had received placed her under enormous pressure to meet the deadline. She practiced extreme discipline, working long hours and using various rituals to spur her writing. She might light candles one night, or pray, or read from one her favorite authors. Sometimes she had to force words onto the page. At other times, she became so immersed in her writing that she lapsed back into her old habit of dreaming she was actually one of her characters.

Her hard work paid off. As the stories developed, Cisneros could see the strong women and girls she had hoped to capture take shape. Determined to write something new, to tell of typical hopes and dreams that blossom in the not-so-typical landscape of the barrio, she persevered. These new stories were connected to one another by a thread, the thread of female strength.

Chapter Six

Fierce Women

After Random House published *Woman Hollering Creek* in 1991, Cisneros no longer had doubts about her future. That same year she won a prestigious $50,000 prize called the Lannan Literary Award for Fiction, awarded annually to exceptional works. Already working on a new book titled *Loose Woman,* Cisneros received another $100,000 advance, this time from Turtle Bay Books. Turtle Bay also issued a new printing of *My Wicked Wicked Ways* because the original publisher, Third Woman Press, had by this point stopped publishing. Having returned to her beloved San Antonio, Cisneros went on tour publicizing her new projects as well as *The House on Mango Street,* which had been reissued by Vintage Press, an imprint of Random House.

Woman Hollering Creek takes up many of the themes from *The House on Mango Street,* expanding on the earlier book's glimpses of life on Chicago's northwest side. Cisneros added new voices to the mix, from migrant Mexican farm workers to factory workers to college graduates. Cisneros wanted to include as many different voices as possible from the Chicano world that so many Americans knew so little about.

Cisneros based the title story of *Woman Hollering Creek* on two Mexican myths that feature a woman who cries out loudly with grief. However, Cisneros updated the story to make the woman's cry one of joy and triumph. The first legend tells of a *Malinche,* or courtesan, believed to be the mother of the Mexican race. It involves Hernando Cortés, the Spanish explorer who invaded Mexico and captured the Aztec Indians in the sixteenth century. In this version, Cortés fathers a son with the *Malinche* and takes the son with him when he returns to Spain. Her cries for her son haunt others with the fear that she will inflict the pain of her own loss on them. The second legend features *La Llorana,* the Weeping Woman. A goddess figure, *La Llorana* is also heard crying at night, having lost her children because her husband cheated on her with other women. Out of great sorrow, *La Llorana* drowns her own children. Both mythical women cry out in anguish over the loss of their children and the treachery of men.

In Cisneros's take on the crying woman tales, the main character keeps her child and leaves the man who makes her miserable. A modern yelling woman helps her do this. "Woman Hollering Creek" tells of this young woman from Mexico named Cleófilas. Filled with hope for a better life, she marries a Mexican American, but she ends up in a dirty American town with a husband who beats her. The thoughts of Cleófilas's father foreshadow the girl's future as the story opens:

> The day Don Serafín gave Juan Pedro Martínez Sánchez permission to take Cleófilas Enriquesta DeLeón Hernández as his bride, across her father's threshold, over several miles of dirt road and several miles of paved, over one border and beyond to a town *en el otro lado*—on the other side—already did he divine the morning his daughter would raise her hand over her eyes, look south, and dream of returning to the chores that never ended, six good-for-nothing brothers, and one old man's complaints. He had said . . . in the hubbub of parting: I am your father, I will never abandon you.

Cleófilas will indeed return home, but only through the help of a community of women.

When a woman's voice cries out in "Woman Hollering Creek," it is strong and assertive, rather than filled with loss or longing. The voice belongs to Felice, whose name means happiness. Felice helps rescue abused women like Cleófilas, along with their children. When Cleófilas, pregnant with her second child, goes for a doctor's visit, the nurse can see that the woman is being abused. The nurse calls Felice, who agrees to drive the pregnant Cleófilas and her child back across the border to Mexico. Everything about Felice seems unusual to Cleófilas. By rescuing women, for instance, Felice fills a role traditionally occupied by men. Felice drives a truck, something Cleófilas thinks of as a man's vehicle; she also curses like a man. Her most unusual behavior of all is when she shouts for no apparent reason when they cross the *arroyo,* or creek, that is named "Woman Hollering." Her triumphant, Tarzan-like shout symbolically replaces the helpless cries of grief that Mexico's traditional mythical women emit. Cisneros does not preach to her readers but offers a glimpse into Mexican culture and mythology that might spark curious readers to learn more about Mexican ways.

In another story from the collection, Cisneros focuses

A sign for the actual "Woman Hollering Creek" along a Texas highway.

on the dangerous stereotypes conveyed by the beloved Barbie doll. With her large bust, tiny waspish waist, and perfectly proportioned hips, the doll has long symbolized ideal physical beauty for American girls. In the late 1960s and the 1970s, feminists voiced concern that such unrealistic models harm the emotional development of young girls, who strive to reach Barbie's impossible ideal. Cisneros uses a Barbie doll to demonstrate that such stereotypes can affect Chicanas even more strongly than Anglos. Not only will young Chicanas long for Barbie's perfect and unreachable body, they will also long to be part of a Barbie culture that, in Cisneros's opinion, rejects them due to their ethnicity.

In the story called "Barbie-Q," Cisneros asks her readers to consider the damage that any stereotype can cause children, whether related to gender or ethnic background. She writes of two young Chicanas who, like other American girls, look to Barbie as a model of femininity. But complicating the issue of gender stereotypes is the fact that, as Chicanas, these girls will never have the idealized pale skin or blond hair of the original Barbie dolls. Finally, living in the poverty that so many Chicanas know, the girls cannot afford to buy the doll or any of her many outfits. Then they come across a "fire sale," where they can afford to buy a Barbie only because she is damaged, with melted hands and feet. They dress the discounted doll in singed clothing, trying to cover her deformities. But no matter how hard they try to disguise her "defects" so that no one will know she is less than perfect, they do not succeed.

The reader realizes that the little girls themselves will always know of the defects, no matter how they cover them up. The girls recognize not only their doll's imperfections, but also what seem, in the Anglo-dominated society they inhabit, to be their own. Cisneros echoes a traditional feminist message that girls who suffer society's rejection for failure to achieve an impossible standard may also reject themselves. She asks readers to consider that, in the case of Chicana girls, their inability to measure up to a requirement for white skin may be the greatest threat to their sense of identity.

As in her previous writing, Cisneros mixes Spanish terms with English, often adding no translation. This technique helps emphasize her ongoing theme of mixed cultural identity. In "Eyes of Zapata," she writes:

> You used to be *tan chistoso. Muy bonachón, muy bromista.* Joking and singing off-key when you had your little drinks. *Tres vicios tengo y los tengo muy arraigados; de ser borracho, jugador, y enamorado.* ... Ay, my life, remember? Always *muy enamorado,* no? Are you still that boy I met at the San Lazaro country fair? Am I still that girl you kissed under the little avocado tree?

Cisneros became so involved with Inés, the main character in that story, that one night she awoke from a dream and for a moment thought that she was Inés. At times like this, Cisneros felt consumed by her character's voices.

Cisneros freely shared her opinion that her stories allowed her to give back to her community. Chicanos and Chicanas could see their lives featured in stories for the first time. But not all of her readers thought she was doing her community a service. After reading one of her stories in the *Los Angeles Times,* one Latino author protested that she belittled her people. Not only did he not like the way that Cisneros portrayed Latinos, he accused her of betrayal. He saw her stories as making fun of Latinos, earning her a great deal of money at the expense of others. Cisneros felt that she did portray Mexican Americans truthfully and multi-dimensionally, faults and all. She blamed his anger on her belief that the newspaper itself featured too few representations of real Mexican Americans.

One way Cisneros would measure reader response to her stories was to try them out on her students. She frequently used her creative writing classes as a testing ground for new works. She knows that she has a good story when she looks into the group and sees every face turned her way, listening intently. Once, she asked a group of students if they had taken notes while listening to her story. Even though they had not, they could repeat the tale back to her in detail. She altered her definition of a good story to be one that people not only want to listen to but can easily recall: "You remember the ones that are important to you or that affect you, and you filter out the ones *que no te sirven,*" that do not mean anything to you.

Cisneros's characters have been labeled "fierce women . . . women of faith" who find a way to survive in challenging worlds. That survival may take place in strange surroundings as the characters immigrate or experience death or disappointment. Yet, they still want to belong, to become a part of something. As the narrator in "Never Marry a Mexican" says, "Human beings pass me on the street, and I want to reach out and strum them as if they were guitars. Sometimes all humanity strikes me as lovely. I just want to reach out and stroke someone, and say There, there, it's all right, honey. There, there, there." Some of the stories in *Woman Hollering Creek* offer readers female characters such as this, who dream in order to survive a harsh reality, who persist in their search for love and self-realization.

One of the *Woman Hollering Creek* stories, "Little Miracles, Kept Promises," brims with diverse voices, as a young woman visits a church where people have posted their prayers in the form of countless letters adhered to the walls. One note states, "Thank you. Our child is born healthy!" In another, the writer relates advice he had been given, that if he "lit a candle every night for seven days and prayed, you maybe could help me with my face breaking out with so many pimples." One note asks simply, "Can you please help me find a man who isn't a pain in the *nalgas*. There aren't any in Texas, I swear. Especially not in San Antonio." Each letter deals with a different problem, each one of crucial importance to the writer who left it there. There are twenty-three letters in all.

Cisneros later explained at a conference in San Antonio that writers must act like ventriloquists, taking on their characters' voices. She collects bits of overheard dialogue and later mixes and shapes those bits to suit her purpose, paying attention to the rhythmic patterns of real-life speech. Sometimes Cisneros searches the San Antonio phone book to come up with names for her characters. Never taking anyone's complete name, she pairs mismatched first and last names for their rhythm, sound, and character. As she told her audience, "real life doesn't have shape. You have to snip and cut." The real world contains many of the raw ingredients, but the writer must select, arrange, and embellish those elements into a well-crafted work of fiction or poetry.

Cisneros once asked a group of Latino and Asian high school students in East Los Angeles what they liked about her stories and poems. They replied, "Cuz you can relate." Her work "is written in a language which they can recognize," Cisneros has said. "It validates them because they see themselves in print for the first time."

Cisneros periodically left San Antonio to teach and write at various schools. She served for a time as writer-in-residence at the University of New Mexico in Albuquerque, the University of Michigan at Ann Arbor, and at the University of California at Irvine and at Berkeley. She not only taught writing classes, she also gave readings that were open to the public. During some presentations, she talked with the audience about her life and her writing, offering tips for navigating the publishing world.

Cisneros once joked that her students are "always sucking my blood." But she added quickly that they could not do that if she did not let them. She referred to her relationship with her students as something founded on an unwritten contract, in which teacher and student both agree to work with and for the other. She continued to feel torn between her own writing and helping her students with their stories. If she worked on her writing over the weekend, she would have to struggle to catch up with her students' stories during the week, sometimes during class: "I read them in class for the first time, and so I have to steal their time in order to be a writer." On the other hand, if she spent all of her time reading and commenting on her students' writing, her "private time gets stolen," leaving her with no time or energy to devote to her own work. For Cisneros, teaching was a constant struggle to find a balance between her obligations to her students and her obligations to herself.

Cisneros's struggle was made more difficult by the attitude of the university administration toward creative activity. The administrators officially encouraged her writing; they wanted her to continue to write and publish while she lectured. Yet, at the same time, they seemed to consider her personal writing an interruption of her academic duties. She had a tough time understanding the mixed signals she was given.

Publication of *Woman Hollering Creek* represented a milestone in Cisneros's career, and also in the world of publishing. With it, Cisneros had crossed over into the mainstream press, and because of this, many more readers would have the chance to encounter her work. A few Chicano writers, such as Gary Soto and Richard Rodriguez, had crossed over into the mainstream previously, but no Chicana had ever done so. In a 1991 interview on National Public Radio, Cisneros remarked that she could not feel truly pleased about her situation as the sole Chicana writer receiving such attention. "I know there are such magnificent writers," she said, "both Latinos and Latinas, both Chicanos and Chicanas," who would never be published by a major publisher like Random House. She hoped her book's success might cause publishers to seek out and find these writers.

In a lengthy 1991 interview with Don Swaim of CBS Radio, Cisneros stated that the "fact that there's a public out there reading is encouraging." She loved the fact that teachers were buying her books. When Swaim remarked that he recently read that only one percent of the adult population of the United States would purchase a hardback book in any given year, Cisneros responded that she understood that many of the very people she hoped to reach with her stories could not afford to buy books. Some of these children would only encounter her stories by hearing a teacher or librarian read them aloud, but even this would make Cisneros happy. She also acknowledged that her work might be considered more "literary" than "popular," meaning it would have a smaller audience and sell fewer copies than well-known blockbusters. As she explained, the money earned by the blockbusters helps to finance smaller projects like her own.

Swaim asked her the familiar question of whether or not *The House on Mango Street* is autobiographical. Cisneros explained, as she had done before, that like most writers of fiction, she "use[s] reality . . . to create a collage" of images that tell stories based at least partially in truth. She explained her choice to use a child, Esperanza, as her narrator by noting that children are good representations of "disempowered" people. To Cisneros's way of thinking, children have "all the spirit that they'll have as an adult," but no voice, and no way to defend themselves. She wanted to provide a voice for them, to act in their defense.

In the interview, Cisneros remembered some especially negative moments from her childhood, including some bad experiences with the nuns she had as teachers. The nuns, she said, were the most "un-Christian" people she had ever met, often embarrassing and harassing the children from poor families. Cisneros admitted that she had only recently regained some semblance of her religious faith, which she had let slip away in response to the nuns' behavior.

Cisneros laughingly referred to herself as a migrant teacher, traveling to different institutions to teach for a few semesters, but always returning to San Antonio as her home base. When Swaim asked what specific advice Cisneros considered crucial for her writing students, she answered, "Don't think so much. Feel!"

Cisneros spoke to Swaim of problems she had encountered with the original printing of *The House on Mango Street*. The publisher had not allowed her to see the book in its final stage before going to press. After the book was released, she discovered that the editors made changes to some of her distinctively worded phrasings, mistakenly believing they were correcting unintentional grammatical errors. The most glaring example of this took place in the book's final sentence, which should read "For the ones who cannot out." The editors had, without Cisneros's knowledge, changed that to read, "For the ones who cannot get out." She made sure the second printing would read as she had intended.

Of the stories in *Woman Hollering Creek,* she named "Eyes of Zapata" as the one she felt the most pride in.

Emiliano Zapata (1879-1919), the Mexican revolutionary who Cisneros had become fascinated with before writing her story "The Eyes of Zapata." He is a legendary figure, revered by many as a defender of Mexico's native culture and poor, agricultural workers. Modern-day rebels in southern Mexico, Zapatistas, take their name from him.

She said that story had evolved out of a fascination with the famous Mexican political revolutionary, Emiliano Zapata. She kept coming across bits of stories involving his first common-law wife, a woman he later abandoned in order to marry another. Cisneros decided to tell the first wife's story as fiction. She wanted the woman to be an equal to Zapata, so she made the character a witch in order to bestow her with great power. In the lengthy story, the woman predicts Zapata's downfall as she recalls the couple's past and tells their future. Cisneros also laughed with Don Swaim over the fact that she was not allowed to choose the title for that book. She had wanted to name it *Milagritas,* meaning little miracles, but her editor would not allow her to use a Spanish title—a rather ironic decision in light of the book's subject matter. Cisneros hoped that one day she would have the stature to choose her own title.

In San Antonio, Cisneros finally did what she had wanted to do for so long—she purchased a house of her own. It was a small Victorian house in a prosperous neighborhood. Later, she would use the house to represent her Mexican heritage, but for now, the house cemented her connection to the city she so loved. She made another significant purchase around this time: a bright red pickup truck that she decorated in typically colorful Mexican style, including hanging fringe around the windshield. The purchase of the truck helped convince her father that she had become successful as a writer. At last, he took her and her vocation seriously.

During one Christmas visit to Chicago, Cisneros spent

time with her sick father. He was bedridden due to a stroke he had recently suffered. She shared one of her stories that had been translated into Spanish with him. Alfredo interrupted his television watching to read the entire story. He laughed at some passages, and some he read aloud, just for the joy of hearing the words. When he finished, he asked Cisneros for copies of the story to hand out to the rest of the family. Cisneros knew then that she had earned her father's approval, something far more important to her than the approval of readers she would never even know.

In 1992, Cisneros traveled to Mexico with several other Latino writers, including Rudolfo Anaya and Carlos Cumpian. Their goal was to introduce their writing to Mexican- and Latin-American readers. While attending the 1992 *Feria Internacional del Libro,* the International Festival of Books, Cisneros joined her fellow writers on a panel discussing their work. On the panel, Cisneros called attention to the sad fact that she was the only Chicana in the world able to support herself with her writing. She issued a challenge to the publishers attending the conference to find and publish work by more women like herself.

Cisneros's writing career seemed now to be more of a sure thing than ever. That year she received two more advances from Random House, one for her poetry collection, *Loose Woman,* and another for a new novel, tentatively titled *Caramelito.*

In a 1990 interview, Cisneros had attributed her success as a teacher and a writer to her willingness to depart from the plan. Sometimes, in order to stimulate a meaningful discussion in her class, she had to allow herself to abandon her lesson plan; at such times she would "get on the track by going off the track." In her writing, too, Cisneros had diverged from the typical "track" laid out for Chicana writers. She had made mistakes early on when she tried to imitate others rather than letting her own voice direct her writing. Finally, she had reached the point where she was moving steadily along the track she had laid out for herself. She declared that when someone has a feeling of being "so solid and so grounded," that person is capable of achieving anything. "You can stand in the middle of the street and cars will go right through you." Cisneros would continue to work such magic.

Chapter Seven

Writer and Activist

As Cisneros continued to tour and speak to students and other groups, she expounded on the themes such as compassion and acceptance that frequently appear in her writing. She stressed the importance of working to build a strong community. She urged her listeners to look around and notice the people who may have been invisible to them before, people like custodians, garbage collectors, and others who perform vital duties for little pay. She encouraged the writers to "help heal the pain" in their communities. One way they could do that was to bring that pain to the attention of a broad reading audience.

Cisneros has said that she takes great pride in being the first of her family's women to speak publicly about social and economic issues. Even though she often focuses on issues pertaining to her own culture, she does reach out to other groups' concerns as well. She considers her speaking out to be an example of the sense of public responsibility she urges other writers to adopt.

In 1992, Cisneros had the opportunity to act on her idealism. A retail clothing chain, the Gap, wanted her to sign on to do several commercials. The offer would have given her exposure, making her a recognizable celebrity and earning her a great deal of money. However, because the Gap never used other Latinos in their ads, Cisneros declined. Had she accepted, she said, she would have felt like a traitor to her ethnic group. She had made herself a representative for Latinos and, as such, had to be careful making decisions like this. Turning down the Gap offer also meant she had to pass up the opportunity to be photographed by noted photographer Annie Leibovitz, who had made a name for herself shooting pictures of Hollywood stars and other famous faces.

In January of 1993, a more personal opportunity for activism arose when Cisneros received a letter from Jasna, her friend from Sarajevo. In the letter, Jasna described the conditions in her war-torn country, where Muslims, Croats, and Serbs battled one another for control of the land. The war destroyed entire villages and killed and maimed countless civilians. Heavy bombing reduced houses and roads to rubble; necessary supplies could not reach those who desperately needed them. Cisneros used her reputation as a writer and social activist to have Jasna's letter published in several major newspapers. Jasna described living conditions that sickened readers. She had no access to bathing facilities or adequate amounts of food. There was no heat during freezing weather, and massive numbers of people were dying from exposure. Those who survived cut down trees along streets and in parks for firewood. Sarajevo had become "a city of grief and pain." The letter appeared in the *New York Times* in early April.

After a few months passed, Cisneros spoke at the International Women's Day Rally in San Antonio. She had one thing on her mind—Jasna's situation. She pleaded with the U.S. government to step in and help the Bosnians, urging the audience and her readers to hear her friend's cries for help. She admitted that she did not know what to do, but she had to try to do something. Over the next several years, until Sarajevo emerged from its war in 1996, Cisneros held prayer meetings for Jasna and her family and friends.

Later in 1993, Cisneros again had another opportunity to act on the courage of her convictions. A bookstore owner in Texas wanted to schedule Cisneros for a reading that would help sell her books. However, when she found out that he had never extended an invitation to a Latino before, she made a demand. In a display of her commitment to the Latino cause, she asked that he invite other Latino writers to join her. Her commitment was rewarded when she won a 1993 Anisfield-Wolf Book Award for her story collection *Woman Hollering Creek.* The award is given out annually to a handful of writers whose work has helped to broaden the public's understanding of and appreciation for the rich diversity of cultures.

In 1994, Cisneros was again able to take advantage of a sudden publishing boom for Latinos. *Publishers Weekly* noted that in the 1990s Latino writers had moved from smaller, lesser-known publishers to bigger publishers with recognizable names. In 1994, Random House published three more of Cisneros's works. Not only did the company reprint *The House on Mango Street* in its original English, it also published a Spanish translation titled *La Casa En Mango* (translated by Elena Poniatowska). They also released a children's book by Cisneros titled *Hairs/Pelitos* for children aged four to eight. Even though she enjoyed her success with Random House, she continued to work with Turtle Bay in order to support smaller publishing houses. The publisher earned money from her books that it could use to help as yet unknown writers of color advance their careers.

As for the writers that Cisneros enjoys reading, she has mentioned Argentine writer Manuel Puig, Mexican Juan Rulfo, and a Spanish writer, Mercè Rodoreda. Cisneros also claims to have been inspired by Asian-American writer Maxine Hong Kingston's *Woman Warrior* to weave myth with reality in her own writing. She mainly reads books published by smaller presses. To Cisneros, these publishers seem more "fearless" about the projects they take on, because they are not concerned with creating a huge blockbuster. Cisneros reads writing that contains what she terms "spiritual content and political content," written by women, minorities, and working-class people.

Cisneros loved being settled in San Antonio. She had told an interviewer previously, "San Antonio is where Latin America begins, and I love it." She especially loved the pervasiveness of Spanish there, the language she

A classic view of San Antonio. In the foreground, the Hall of Performing Arts is decorated with a Mexican-inspired tile mosaic. The Tower of the Americas, built for the 1968 World's Fair, looms over the theater and the rest of downtown.

grew up hearing her father speak. She has stated, "Everywhere I go I get ideas, something of the language, something in the people's expressions, something in the rhythm of their saying something in Spanish." Her readers could count on that "something" showing up in her stories and poetry. San Antonio's Tejano culture, with its combination of Texan and Mexican influence, greatly appealed to her.

By 1995, Cisneros had gained unprecedented fame

and respect. That year she received a prestigious award from the MacArthur Foundation in the amount of $225,000. MacArthur fellowships, popularly called "genius grants," are awarded annually to individuals deemed to have demonstrated exceptional creativity, accomplishment, and promise. The fellowship allows the recipient time and money to actively continue their creative work. Cisneros could use the grant in any way she pleased. Combined with her publishing and public speaking income (she would soon command $10,000 for public presentations), she had achieved financial freedom. However, she had vowed never to forget her impoverished beginnings in the barrio.

Critics have viewed Cisneros's use of language and her ideas regarding owning one's own space as important metaphors for the theme of independence. Bilingualism, the speaking of two languages, remains crucial to her stories and poetry. In her first major work, *The House on Mango Street,* the double languages represent the boundaries of the double worlds Esperanza moves back and forth between. As she travels between these worlds, she creates a new territory made up of both cultures. The idea of space, whether literal, as in the sense of a house, or symbolic, in the sense of cultures, remains of vital importance in Cisneros's writing. The use of language and the physical place the characters inhabit combine to represent their status in society. Throughout much of Cisneros's writing, languages and houses symbolize the characters and their situations in life. When they control their language and their space, they attain independence.

Cisneros soon began public readings of her novel-in-progress, which she had begun to call *Caramelo*. Many who heard her read thought that this novel would be the one that would propel her to worldwide fame and make her name a household word. Then, tragedy interrupted her work when her father, Alfredo Cisneros, died on February 12, 1996. Her grief over his death caused her to suffer a serious case of writer's block. She put her novel aside for a time and would not read publicly from it again until 2002.

In the meantime, she unintentionally found another way to attract attention to the Chicano community. Cisneros's wealthy San Antonio neighbors were not pleasantly surprised when, in May 1997, she decided to paint her Victorian cottage a vivid purple. Because bright colors such as purples, greens, reds, oranges, and pinks are typically used in Mexico, Cisneros felt these colors would be appropriate to use in a neighborhood that inhabited land once owned by Mexico. It was her way of celebrating the rich history of San Antonio that united Anglos and Mexicans. But the color shocked the members of the prestigious King William Historic District, which had rules regarding appropriate colors for the neighborhood homes. Some praised the cottage's varied shades of amethyst, lilac, and violet, but for most of the district's inhabitants, the color did not measure up to the neighborhood's strict regulations. As a community that finds great symbolic importance in historic structures—consider the Alamo, for instance, and the numerous Spanish missions that dot the city—San Antonio took

Cisneros's departure from the rules quite seriously.

Situated only a half mile from the Alamo, on the San Antonio River, the King William district had been settled by wealthy German immigrants in 1860s. The idyllic neighborhood became known for its impressive houses shaded by massive pecan and cypress trees. In the early 1900s, the area started to decline, but by the 1950s, restoration had begun, and the neighborhood quickly regained its earlier stature. It has again become a fashionable place to live and many prominent local celebrities and businessmen reside there. The San Antonio Historic Design and Review Commission, made up of architects, historians, and other experts, governs restoration in the district. The commission's goal is to protect the original look of the area and to maintain its historic accuracy. In 1995, only two years before Cisneros painted her house purple, the board had faced trouble when it approved a bright red color for the city's new library. But Cisneros's choice of vivid purple, which she felt aligned her with her culture's love for bright colors, did not receive the board's approval.

The neighborhood split over its attitude toward Cisneros's color choice. One group, nicknamed the "Sandranistas," supported Cisneros and backed up the accusations of racism she made against the historic commission. Another group opposed her move and labeled her an egotistical "grandstanding publicity seeker." Passions ran high on all sides. Cisneros's actions recalled Esperanza's statement from *The House on Mango Street,* "One day I'll own my own house, but I won't forget who

I am or where I came from." In 1997, Esperanza's voice had been heard by millions of readers and over 500,000 copies of the novel had sold. It had become required reading material in college courses from Yale to Stanford. Cisneros's readers heard of the house-painting controversy and could understand her actions.

This was not the first time Cisneros had offended some of her neighbors. At one point, she had placed a sign in her yard reading "We Love Trolleys," referring to the sightseeing trolleys that had begun to regularly bring tourists through the exclusive neighborhood. A favorite sight was Cisneros's newly purple house. Many of King William's inhabitants did not care for the trolleys—or for Cisneros's attitude.

Cisneros submitted a research paper to the board in which she argued that she should be allowed to use the bright shades favored by her people, because these colors are an important part of Texas's history, a history that is entwined with Mexico's. The board, however, responded that they based the historic significance of house paint in King William on three specific criteria. Residents could choose a color which: "(1) at one time graced the home; (2) appeared on at least one other home in the historic district; or (3) can be shown to have been in general use" during the time that the original houses were constructed. Not only had no house ever been painted purple, the paint color that Cisneros chose, "Corsican Purple," had been manufactured for only twenty years. Had her house been located just a short distance away, Cisneros explained, the conflict would have never occurred. Her

Sandra Cisneros in San Antonio in 2002. *(AP Photo/Eric Gay.)*

house sits just inside the historic district's boundary.

Cisneros countered by using other historic records. She called attention to the lack of records regarding the poorer districts of the city. No records existed that traced the development of shantytowns and tract houses. She declared, "We are a people *sin papeles* ("without papers)!" adding, "We don't exist." The dispute was not about her house, she said, but rather "the entire Tejano community." The commission did not agree. One member told her she had no convincing argument to make her case, she simply wanted her house to be purple. The commission went on that this was not a political or cultural issue but simply a complaint by one homeowner who did not want to follow the same rules everyone else abided by. The commission did agree that she might paint her house a bright pink, as one historical residence already bore that traditional Tejano color. Cisneros ended by stating she would not back down. She would continue to push the commission to expand "its vision to include the history and the color palette of the Tejano people."

Later in August, Cisneros staged an interview in her front yard and invited the national media to attend. She dressed for the dramatic presentation, donning a purple dress and sitting in a purple chair in her front yard. Even her dog wore a purple bandana. When a trolley stopped in front of her house and the driver asked whether his riders might take pictures, Cisneros agreed. She smiled and asked each person who snapped a picture to take a copy of a petition, which she had printed on purple paper and placed on a clipboard that hung from her gate. Be sure to "mail them to the mayor," she told her visitors. "It's not about my house. It's about history." Before long, purple ribbons began showing up, tied around neighborhood trees in an expression of solidarity with Cisneros.

A CNN correspondent named Maria Hinojosa interviewed Cisneros about the situation. Critics argued that the reporter asked only friendly questions, avoiding more difficult ones, such as why the author had chosen to live in one of the most exclusive neighborhoods in the city, rather than taking up residence in one of the poorer sections she claimed to support. They wanted to know why she had wanted to live in a historic area with clearly publicized rules if she was not willing to abide by them.

By this point, Cisneros had earned a reputation for doing as she pleased. When the *Texas Monthly* magazine first requested an interview with her in 1995, Cisneros agreed to the interview, but only if it was done by a Latina author of her choice. The magazine refused, citing its own editorial integrity. Cisneros retaliated by refusing to grant *Texas Monthly* an interview in connection with the purple house uproar. Her agent told the editors that Cisneros could not cooperate "with a magazine that printed so few works by Hispanic writers."

San Antonio would not back down in the house controversy. Although Cisneros had agreed to paint the house the accepted shade of pink, she did not make any immediate moves to do so. On August 6, 1997, the commission agreed to waive its fine for a code violation, a fine that could run as high as $1000 each day. The issue would not be resolved until October of 1998, when the commission requested that Cisneros bring in a sample of the paint from her house, so they could see how it had been altered by two years of Texan sunshine. Using a diplomatic approach, the commission conceded that the color had faded to violet and was now an acceptable historical color. Cisneros claimed it had been periwinkle all along, and that the San Antonio authorities should never have raised the issue. She had recently acquired a new office, and she made a point of musing publicly about which color she might use on that building. She joked that she might choose mango, adding, "I don't know why some paint company hasn't snatched me up to be spokes-woman for their new Tejano palette!" She stated that she might write a book about the house paint controversy. Laughing, she claimed it would be a coloring book.

Some people approved of Cisneros's methods of drawing attention to the Chicano community, while others did not. Regardless of public opinion, she had no intention of changing her ways.

Chapter Eight

Keeping the Faith

While Sandra Cisneros no longer wanted to live in Chicago, she returned there often to visit her family. She also remained involved in Chicago's Latino community. She visited the Duncan YMCA in Chicago's Near West Side neighborhood to participate in its literary program, the Writer's Voice. When the program ran into problems, with some writers complaining of poor treatment by the center, the executive director decided to make changes. It became the only Chicago YMCA to dedicate itself to the arts. At a ribbon-cutting ceremony on November 19, 1997, the new Chernin Center for the Arts was opened. Serving three Chicago Housing Authority complexes and an area around the University of Illinois, the center offered tennis and outdoor basketball programs, but the arts remained its primary focus. Cisneros agreed with the executive director, who stated that the arts and communication programs helped "to build self-esteem and pride in our young people."

On March 3, 1998, Cisneros participated in a radio interview with personality Amy Goodman. Goodman gave Cisneros the chance to discuss one of her favorite topics: why she decided to become a writer. Cisneros explained that as a child, she mainly wanted to have her name in the library card catalog. She laughed when Goodman reminded her that many library catalogs are now on computer. Fortunately for Cisneros, she knew of a few small-town Texas libraries that retained their dog-eared flip files. She also took the opportunity to make a political statement in favor of the National Endowment for the Arts (NEA). She stressed the importance of the NEA, a program that is often criticized by politicians who want to reduce the funding for the NEA and more tightly control how their funds are spent.

Cisneros stressed that her two NEA grants were important to her beyond the financial assistance they provided. She recalled that when she received her first NEA grant, she desperately needed reminding that she was a writer because most of her time was spent on teaching assignments that left her little time for her art. Receiving the grant reminded her that her writing mattered; it also made it possible for her to complete *The House on Mango Street.* As well, the grant provided her the opportunity to travel to Bosnia and other parts of Europe. That trip had changed her life. The second grant came along at a time she was "hanging by my fingernails," just barely paying her bills. In the interview, she emphasized that U.S. citizens should value, and continue to help to fund, creative work because of its power to inspire and educate.

Cisneros continued her writing and lecturing, appearing in venues across the country. *The House on Mango Street* appeared as a book-on-tape in 1998, read by Cisneros herself. One reviewer wrote that Cisneros could not have chosen a better reader: "her pitch is perfect, her rhythm is rollicking, and the language is always refreshingly honest and wise." She also contributed to a collection titled *Short Fiction on Faith,* published that same year by Beacon Press. Her story, along with those by Leslie Marmon Silko, E. M. Forster, Isaac Bashevis Singer, and others, focused on the nature of faith and how it functions in everyday lives. Southern Methodist University Press included her story "Barbie-Q" in its 1998 collection, *Texas Bound, Book II: 22 Texas Stories.* Designed as a fundraiser, the book's sales benefit the Dallas Museum of Art.

Later in 1998, Cisneros joined fellow Latina author Ana Castillo and eight other recipients who were honored by the Mexican Fine Arts Center Museum in Chicago. The museum presented the awards as part of the Sor Juana Festival, which celebrates seventeenth-century Mexican poet Sor Juana Inés de la Cruz, considered one of the greatest lyric poets of the colonial era. The festival hosts an annual exhibit of Mexican and Mexican-American arts, and honors five outstanding women whose work has had an impact on the city of Chicago.

Part of Cisneros's mission continued to be helping other writers, including teachers. When teacher Greg Michie wrote a book, *Holler If You Hear Me: The Education of a Teacher and His Students,* about his experiences in Chicago's secondary schools, Cisneros agreed to write the foreword. In it, she tells of meeting Michie and his students after she accepted an invitation from them to visit their school. She had responded to their letter, one of many such invitations that she received, in part because she could see herself in the young writers. She mused about the young working-class women, "daughters of mexicanos," whose home life she imagined to include "the linoleum-covered flat they rented, the formica [sic] kitchen table" used for their homework, "a radio chattering nervously in the kitchen," the continuous song from the passing ice cream truck, and winter's "terrible dark" that she compared to a "velvet theater curtain" falling. Acting upon the strong sense of connection she felt, Cisneros committed to visiting Michie's class. When she arrived, the students treated her like a celebrity.

Like many other Americans, Cisneros has worried for years about the country's educational system. Being in the Chicago school reminded her of her own school experience. She did not feel comfortable inside the building and confessed to always feeling like an eleven-year-old child when she entered a school. She toured Michie's tiny, narrow classroom and was impressed with his passion for art, music, and drama. Most of all, he impressed her with his willingness to leave his own culture and take an interest in that of the barrio.

Four years after the visit, Michie and some of his students were among the group that attended a reading Cisneros gave at Chicago's Mexican Fine Arts Center. Since that time, the students had gained admission to college, and Cionseros credited their enthusiastic teacher for encouraging them to do so. She concluded her foreword to Michie's book by writing, "It is a great and marvelous thing to be reminded that to change the world we need only to change ourselves. Greg Michie and his students give me that hope."

Increasingly well-known, Cisneros represented her people in numerous capacities. As a member of an ethnic minority, her opinion was sought regarding presidential candidates. In 1998, her home-state governor, George W. Bush of Texas, had made clear that he would seek the 2000 Republican nomination. Because Cisneros lived in San Antonio, she drew attention from one reporter who quoted her as having said "some Hispanics are charmed by the governor's Spanish speaking." The *Chicago Tribune* reported Cisneros's remarks as those of a Chicago native. Bush had made certain that the country understood he considered himself bilingual, a special point of pride as governor of a state containing so many Spanish-speaking voters. Cisneros's remarks seemed to support the conservative governor; this surprised many people, as her own liberal views were widely known. Besides that, few would truly consider Governor Bush's minimal grasp of Spanish as bilingualism. Within days, the *Tribune* had to withdraw its report, entering a message in its "Corrections and Clarifications Section." There it informed readers that Cisneros's further remarks had mistakenly been omitted, leaving some readers with "the erroneous impression that she endorses Bush." In actuality, she had said "that for Bush to confront the many serious issues concerning Hispanics, you're going to need a lot more than 'omo esta usted?'" (That phrase is Spanish for "How are you?" and is one of the first to be learned in any Spanish class.) Her statement suggested that Bush lacked an understanding of Hispanics, regardless of his professed language skills, and he would need to do much work if he hoped to gain the support of the Spanish-speaking community.

When Cisneros appeared as featured speaker at the 1999 Distinguished Latino Scholar Forum, hosted by the San Jose Center for Latino Arts and the San Jose State University Center for Literary Arts in California, she dressed in native garb and wore an orange flower in her long braided hair. Cisneros told the story of her first memory of the importance of language to her writing. She spoke of how she was first drawn to the common language spoken by working class men and women, the vernacular, when she encountered local farmers when she was in Iowa for graduate school. "It was great joy for me to use their speech in my writing," she explained. "It was good to hear a different voice than that of my professors or fellow students." Later in the talk, she shared excerpts from her novel *Caramelo,* which she had returned to working on.

In September of 1999, a book titled *Smokestacks & Skyscrapers*, edited by David Starkey and Richard Guzman, was published. It included excerpts from Cisneros's writing. The book features 114 selections of memoir, fiction, drama, poetry, and essays about Chicago from more than seventy writers spanning the seventeenth century to the twentieth. It begins with the words of a Potawatomi chief, speaking to the Chicago Council, and continues with writing by Theodore Dreiser, Upton Sinclair, Edna Ferber, David Mamet, and Richard Wright. Cisneros's piece leads readers down Maxwell Street, emphasizing the ethnic mix of its inhabitants. Even though she had moved from Chicago, the city continued to claim her as one of its own. Around this time, her poetry also appeared in an anthology of up-and-coming-writers, *Boomer Girls* (University of Iowa Press).

Cisneros continued her activism by lending her name to the campaign against capital punishment. In November of 2000, she was one of a dozen writers, including Joan Didion, E. L. Doctorow, William Styron, and Kurt Vonnegut, who printed an open letter to President Clinton on the topic. The letter focused on one federal prisoner, Juan Raul Garza, whose execution was scheduled to take place in one month, on December 12. Convicted of murder, Garza would be the first federal prisoner executed since John Kennedy's administration in the 1960s.

The letter made the point that almost seventy-five percent of prisoners selected by the federal government for execution are minorities. It also pointed out that Garza, a Hispanic, had been handed a much stiffer penalty than whites who had committed the same crime. The group asked Clinton to commute the sentence to life in prison without possibility for release. The letter added, "Short of that step, we ask you to impose a moratorium on federal executions." Clinton had already postponed the execution once, and he did so again in December, citing the need for further study of the facts of the case. Garza's stay was shortlived, however, and he was executed the following June under the administration of George W. Bush. Cisneros continued to work towards putting an end to capital punishment.

In another anthology, published in 2001, excerpts from several chapters in *The House on Mango Street* appeared. The collection, titled *Growing Up Poor: A Literary Anthology,* edited by Robert Coles and Randy Testa, includes poems, stories, and essays that focus on poverty. The editors wrote that Cisneros could easily identify with her main character, Esperanza, because she had grown up "rat poor." A child psychiatrist and noted author, Coles agreed with the writers that literature holds "reservoirs of wisdom" that might be used to rescue those who suffer poverty, if only temporarily. He gathered the stories together in the hopes that they might "offer a certain richness" to those who suffer from a lack of everyday necessities. Among the other celebrated authors included in the collection are Zora Neale Hurston, Raymond Carver, Langston Hughes, and Sherman Alexie. *Growing up Poor* has been praised as a poweful collection that offers insight into the world of poverty.

In October of 2001, Chicagoans thought of Cisneros as they deliberated over which book would be selected for the city's "One Book, One Chicago" project. The project aims to unite people from across the city as they read and discuss the selected book. To be chosen for the project a book had to meet only two requirements: it had to be readable by teenagers as well as their parents, and it had to be in print. In 2000, Harper Lee's *To Kill a Mockingbird* had been adopted by the public library as the project's first book. The project emphasized uniting Chicagoans into one reading community, as the book was discussed citywide in newspaper articles, in classrooms, and at special library presentations. When the time came to choose the 2001 book, readers made dozens of suggestions to the Library Commissioner. One *Chicago Tribune* reporter listed his own suggestions, including *The House on Mango Street*. He described the book as "Poetic, seemingly simple yet deceptively powerful," adding that "for Hispanics, it's a mirror of their experience. For non-Hispanics, it's a window into an aspect of American life frequently misunderstood." Ultimately the city did not choose Cisneros's book, but the fact that the once-poor Chicago resident's book was considered a possibility was an honor in itself.

Cisneros's public appearances continued, and in November 2001 she spoke at the University of California at Berkeley as part of the campus celebration of the Mexican holiday the Day of the Dead. She noted what a special time it was for people with multicultural backgrounds like her own, "people who are in between." Stressing that multicultural groups must work to have their communities understood, Cisneros warned that all of us stand to lose if this understanding is not reached. For the occasion, Cisneros had written an essay titled "An *Ofrenda* (offering) for My Father on Day of the Dead." In it she relates the story of her father's death and concludes that, for her, the Spanish language has allowed

Day of the Dead, or *Dia de los Muertos,* celebrations center around the belief that deceased loved ones will return to visit their families. Favorite foods are prepared, candles are lit, and cemeteries overflow with colorful flowers to welcome the beloved guests. Candy, toys, and artwork in the form of playful skeletons and skulls also appear around this holiday, which falls on November 2, the same day the Catholic Church celebrates All Souls' Day.

her to preserve her past and her childhood culture. "With my father's death the thread that links me to my other self, to my other language was severed," she told the audience.

Like others with ties to the Mexican community, Cisneros works to keep that culture a vital part of her life. In her opinion, the Anglo culture in the U.S. often pressures immigrants to drop their old ways in order to assimilate into the dominant, hybrid culture. In her speech at Berkeley, she discussed topics such as love and drug abuse in addition to death. She related her own past bouts of alcohol abuse. She interprets such self-abuse as an attempt to avoid feeling isolated in a culture that does not always value her heritage. Then she praised poetry as a solution: "The great thing about poetry . . . is you're supposed to feel. It can ease the evil out of your heart." One audience member said she had been reading Cisneros's work since grade school, and that her poetry and stories made the young woman proud to be Latino.

At the University of California at Irvine on April 10, 2002, Cisneros read from the soon-to-be-published *Caramelo*. (The novel was by this time scheduled for an October 2002 release by Knopf, a division of Random House.) Of the reading, a student reporter wrote, "It was apparent that the audience was enraptured—and left wanting to hear more." The title of Cisneros's presentation, "All Parts from Mexico, Made in the USA," came from the title of one of the novel's chapters. The student introducing Cisneros praised her work for its power to make readers question their views of themselves and the world they inhabit. In *Caramelo,* boundaries of all sorts are crossed and navigated: the emotional boundaries between family members as well as geographical boundaries that separate friends and families. A folk saga, *Caramelo* features the experiences of Mexican migrants told from the point of view of a curious little girl who learns of her heritage from her grandmother.

Audience members noted Cisneros's sincerity as she replied to audience questions following her reading. She admitted that political issues often inspire her nonfiction and fiction, but that she bases her poetry on sentiment rather than logic. Publication is not what motivates her to write, she claimed. Rather it is the opportunity to learn something about herself or her community that keeps her writing. She advised those who aspire to write to "imagine what you say is so dangerous, it can't be published." If the writer does this, she will not be distracted by the idea of publication, nor will she waste time writing about unimportant topics. Cisneros also encouraged reading voraciously, noting that she reads her favorite authors' works repeatedly, "as if she were an apprentice." Continuing her busy circuit of talks, Cisneros appeared days later as the main speaker the Texas Writers Conference at Schreiner University in Kerrville, Texas.

In October 2002, Cisneros returned to Chicago, a place that always filled her with emotion. As she stated in an interview with the *Chicago Tribune,* she grew up in a part of the city that tourists do not visit and postcards do not portray. When she sees her old neighborhood, she admits to feeling "sad . . . defeated . . . in despair," mainly because she recalls the struggles of all of its inhabitants. In a homecoming of her own, however, she agreed to begin her twenty-city book tour celebrating *Caramelo's* publication in her home city by taking part in Chicago's annual Book Festival. She staged two readings, one at a Latino community center, another in a bookstore called Women and Children First. Her publisher, Knopf, felt particularly optimistic regarding the potential for high sales and printed a first run of 150,000 hardback copies of the four-hundred-plus-page novel.

While Cisneros retains bad memories of her childhood in Chicago, she remained gracious and friendly with her readers there, agreeing to pose for photographs as she signed copies of her novel. At the bookstore signing, she exhibited her well-known free spirit, removing her decorative wrap to uncover a less-than-flattering blouse that revealed

Sandra's unhappy memories of childhood in Chicago did not keep her from returning to the city fairly regularly. She even began her publicity tour of *Caramelo* there. *(Photograph by David Head, Jr. © 2005.)*

her full figure. "It's one of my favorites," she laughed, shrugging away the amused looks of her fans. Each of her returns to Chicago provides an excuse for a family reunion, and this time, too, she enjoyed spending time with her mother, who lives in suburban Lombard, and her brothers, who all reside in various parts of the city. She still feels the loss of her father, and she dedicated *Caramelo* to him: "Para ti, Papá."

With *Caramelo,* Cisneros returned to the themes of family and place. Critical reception of the novel was overwhelmingly positive. The review appearing in the *New York Times* starts out by saying that "Sandra Cisneros has written a joyful, fizzy novel, a deliciously subversive reminder that 'American' applies to plenty of territory beyond the borders of the United States." A journalist from *Women's Review of Books* wrote that reviewers like herself would have "to find the words with which to sing this novel's praises . . . *Caramelo* is superb," though she added that some readers will likely be distracted by the footnotes appearing throughout the novel.

Like Cisneros's first novel twenty years earlier, *Caramelo* employs the narrative voice of a young girl who is seven years old when the book begins and a grown woman by the time it concludes. Autobiographical aspects are revealed when readers learn that Celaya, nicknamed "Lala," is, like Cisneros, the only girl in a family with seven children. Another thing Lala shares with Cisneros is a belief in the importance of telling stories. She learns her stories from her family and passes them on. Storytelling forms the focus of the book from its opening epigram, *"Cuentame algo, aunque sea una mentira,"* or "Tell me a story, even if it's a lie."

In eighty-six chapters, Lala tells many stories with a huge cast of characters, including family members: Awful Grandmother, Uncle Fat-Face, Uncle Baby, her six brothers, a cousin named Elvis and one named Aristotle, and her father, Inocencio Reyes, who, like Cisneros's own father, upholsters furniture for a living. Cisneros

The cover of Sandra Cisneros's long-awaited novel, *Caramelo* (Knopf). When it was published in October 2002, the book was greeted with universal praise. *(The cover of* Caramelo *reproduced courtesy of Random House/Knopf.)*

uses all of the characters to tell the story of Lala's family and its migration from Mexico to the United States. Lala, who matures as the stories progress, must eventually write the story of her own life.

The novel's title comes from Lala's great-great-grandmother's talent as a weaver who produced Mexican shawls, or *rebozos,* made of every fabric imaginable, from plain cotton to elegant silk. The term *caramelo*

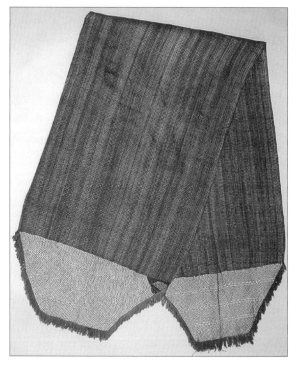

Rebozos have been worn as protective and decorative wraps by women all around the world. Popularized in Spain during the time of Islamic rule, *rebozos* were brought to the Americas during the Spanish colonial period. They can be used as coverings for the head or face, as shawls or aprons, or to carry a baby.

describes a special rebozo made of silk, colored gold and tan with black and white flecks. Readers are reminded on every page of Cisneros's talent as a poet, as she makes deft use of imagery, metaphor, and magical realism. The words flow as smoothly as the liquid caramel candy suggested by the grandmother's rebozo. Cisneros peppers the tale with abundant passages in Spanish, only translating some of these to English. (Much of the rest can be loosely understood through context.)

Caramelo is a sprawling, nonlinear narrative made up of interrelated stories that Cisneros skillfully weaves together, like a rebozo, through the voice of the narrator, Celaya Reyes, or "Lala" as she is called. As Cisneros describes it, "I've always thought that my literary antecedents were not writers but weavers. . . . What is telling a story but keeping track of those threads?" The book traces Lala's life as she journeys with her family between Mexico, Chicago, and San Antonio, relaying her family's stories and the larger history they are a part of. Cisneros uses footnotes throughout the novel, sometimes to translate Spanish passages, other times to offer bits and pieces of Mexican and Mexican-American history, or to cite poetry or song lyrics; still other footnotes allow Cisneros to interject her own commentary on these and other matters. The footnotes serve as disruptions and elucidations, and further confirm for the reader that *Caramelo* is not an ordinary novel that will proceed from beginning to end along a linear path. All of these loose threads work together to tell Lala's story.

One of the novel's characters is Awful Grandmother,

Sandra Cisneros writing in her San Antonio home. *(Photograph courtesy of John Dyer, © John Dyer, 2005.)*

and it is she who gives Lala her stories. After suffering rejection by her boyfriend, Lala wanders about her grandmother's house in Mexico, ties the caramelo rebozo under her chin, and begins to suck on the fringe. In the magic of poetry, the fringe sustains Lala by filling her with hope and faith and feeding a later epiphany that occurs as Lala stands outside of a church: "honest to God, this sounds like a lie, but it's true. The universe a cloth, and all humanity interwoven. Each and every person connected to me, and me connected to them, like the strands of a *rebozo*. Pull one string and the whole thing comes undone. Each person who comes into my life affecting the pattern, and me affecting theirs." This is the prevailing message of *Caramelo,* that our humanity connects us, despite differences in skin color, religion, or birthplace, and that we all must tell our own stories to deepen that connection.

Cisneros's poetry and fiction continues to have a great influence. Not only does she represent individuals whose voices have not been widely heard, she also offers a chance for all readers, regardless of ethnic background, to meet those individuals, perhaps learning from them along the way. Critics agree that she is important on several levels. She is one of the first Latina writers to be so extensively published in English, the first Latina writer to earn a six-figure advance for a projected book. She continues to garner praise and awards, simultaneously remaining loyal to her political and cultural heritage. By combining poetic elements in her fiction and mixing Spanish voices with English ones, Cisneros has created a richly textured narrative that charms her readers while challenging them to embrace difference and learn from it.

Believing that with fame comes responsibility, Cisneros declares that she will never take lightly her role as a representative of the Latino community. She has said that as a writer who matured without culturally relevant writing models, "she felt impoverished with nothing of personal merit to say." Sandra Cisneros has made sure that the next generation of writers will not share that dilemma.

Timeline

1954   On December 20, in Chicago, Illinois, Sandra Cisneros is born to Alfredo and Elvira Cisneros.

1959   Begins school.

1966   Moves into the first house her family has owned, in a poor neighborhood in south Chicago.

1968-
1972   Attends all-girl Josephinum Catholic High School; has her first publication in the school's literary journal, which she also edits.

1972   Enrolls in Loyola University, Chicago.

1976   Graduates Loyola; enters University of Iowa Writers' Workshop.

1978   Graduates from University of Iowa with MFA in creative writing.

1978-
1981   Works as counselor at Latino Youth Alternative High School in Chicago; poetry included in Chicago Transit Authority's poetry project; meets fellow Mexican-American writer Gary Soto.

1980   Her chapbook, *Bad Boys,* is published.

1982-
1983   Receives first NEA grant; works to complete *The House on Mango Street;* residency at Michael Karolyi Artist's Foundation in Venice, Italy; writes poems for *My Wicked Wicked Ways;* meets lifelong friend Jasna K.

1984   *Mango Street* is published to positive reviews; Cisneros moves to San Antonio, Texas.

1985   Receives the Before Columbus American Book Award

for *Mango Street;* receives Dobie-Paisano Fellowship.

1987 Returns to Chicago; *My Wicked Wicked Ways* published; visiting professor at California State University at Chico; receives second NEA grant; *Mango Street* and *Woman Hollering Creek* sold to Random House/Vintage Press.

1991 *Woman Hollering Creek* published and awarded the PEN Center West Award for Best Fiction of 1991; Cisneros receives Lannan Literary Award.

1992 Receives advance from Random House for a new novel; continues to have her essays, poems, and stories published in numerous magazines, journals, and anthologies.

1993 Becomes peace activist for sake of Jasna K.; *Woman Hollering Creek* wins the Anisfield-Wolf Award for excellence in literature of diversity.

1994 Poetry collection *Loose Woman* published; her children's book *Hairs/Pelitos* is published.

1995 Receives a MacArthur "genius grant" Fellowship; Spanish translation of *Mango Street* published.

1997 Father dies on February 12; sparks debate in San Antonio when she paints her house purple.

1998 Honored with a lifetime achievement award from the Mexican Fine Arts Center Museum, Chicago; audio version of *Mango Street* appears with Cisneros as reader; has stories included in more anthologies.

1999 More of her writing is anthologized.

2000 Works to end capital punishment.

2001 *Mango Street* is candidate for Chicago's "One Book, One Chicago" project; excerpts from *Mango Street* included in the anthology *Growing Up Poor.*

2002 Cisneros presents public readings from her forthcoming novel, *Caramelo,* which is published by Knopf in October to enthusiastic reviews.

2003 Continues community work as a fundraiser and advisor to community organizations; works on a new collection of stories.

Sources

CHAPTER ONE: Born into Two Cultures

p. 12, "about third-floor flats . . ." Sandra Cisneros, "Ghosts and Voices: Writing from Obsession," *The Americas Review,* vol. 15, no.1, Spring 1987, 70.

p. 14, "simple and much more . . ." Wolfgang Binder, ed., *Partial Autobiogaphies: Interview with Twenty Chicano Poets* (Erlangen: Verlag, Palm & Enke, 1985), 54.

p. 15, "I am the only daughter . . ." Sandra Cisneros, "Only Daughter," *Glamour,* November 1990, 256.

p. 15, "in intelligence . . ." Binder, *Partial Autobiogaphies,* 56.

p. 16, "I never had to charge. . ." Ibid., 69.

p. 16, "Puccini opera . . . sadness and her rolling pin" Sandra Cisneros, "Notes to a Young(er) Writer," *The Americas Review,* vol. 15, no. 1, Spring 1987, 75.

p. 16, "Thus clutching . . ." Cisneros, "Ghosts," 70.

p. 16, "vitamins" Cisneros, "Notes," 74.

p. 17, "returned like the tides" Binder, *Partial Autobiogaphies,* 55.

p. 17, "on the living room . . ." Pilar E. Rodriguez Aranda,"On the Solitary Fate of Being Mexican, Female, Wicked and Thirty-three: An Interview with Sandra Cisneros," *The Americas Review,* vol. 15, no. 1, Spring 1987, 66.

p. 18, "I grew up with . . ." Sheila Benson, "From the Barrio to the Brownstone," *Los Angeles Times,* May 7, 1991, F1.

p. 18, "the fierce language . . . language of tenderness" Harryette Romell Mullen, "'A Silence Between us Like a Language':

The Untranslatability of Experience in Sandra Cisneros's *Woman Hollering Creek," Melus,* vol. 21, Summer 1996, 3-20.

p. 19, "Good lucky . . . tum-tum up good" Cisneros, "Ghosts," 72.

p. 19, "When did I talk . . ." Cisneros, "Notes," 74.

p. 20, "that kind" and *"gente baja"* Cisneros, "Ghosts," 71.

p. 21, "straddling the . . . middle ground" Aranda, "On the Solitary Fate," 68.

CHAPTER TWO: From Duckling to Swan

p. 22, "the buildings smelled . . . belly with fear." Sandra Cisneros, Foreword, *Holler if You Hear Me: The Education of a Teacher and His Students*, Gregory Michie (New York: Teachers College Press, 1999), xi.

p. 23, "big, hulky . . ." Ibid., x.

p. 25, "Mom! The kids . . ." Aranda, "On the Solitary Fate," 79.

p. 25, "into love . . ." Sandra Cisneros, "Guadalupe: the Sex Goddess," *Ms.* vol. 7, no. 1, July 1996, 44.

p. 26, "was ready to sacrifice . . ." Ibid.

p. 27, "filled . . . with pleas for . . ." Binder, *Partial Autobiogaphies,* 63.

p. 30, "What could I know?. . ." Cisneros, "Ghosts," 72.

p. 30, "A balloon tied to an achor . . ." Ibid., 9.

p. 32, "It was not until this moment . . ." Aranda, "On the Solitary Fate," 65.

p. 32, "This is how . . ." Binder, *Partial Autobiogaphies,* 63.

p. 34, "if Emily . . ." Aranda, "On the Solitary Fate," 75.

CHAPTER THREE: Like Pearls on a Necklace

p. 36, "meter and metaphor . . ." Cisneros, *Holler if You Hear,* ix.

p. 37, "drank and drugged . . ." Ibid.

p. 38, "man, could they talk . . ." Ibid.

p. 39, "too timid . . . disappear" Ibid., xi.

p. 39, "house in the suburbs" Cisneros, "Notes," 75.

p. 40, "he wasn't Mexican . . ." Ibid.

p. 40, "the seams showing" Feroza Jussawalla and Reed Way

Dasenbrock, *Interview with Writers of the Post-Colonial World* (Jackson: University Press of Mississippi, 1992), 290.

p. 41, "best buddy . . . pieces in the book" Cisneros, "Do You Know Me? I Wrote *The House on Mango Street*," *The Americas Review,* vol. 15, no. 1, Spring 1987, 78-79.

p. 42, "We didn't always . . . moving a lot" Cisneros, *The House on Mango Street* (New York: Random House, 1987), 3.

p. 42, "But what I remember . . ." Ibid.

p. 43, "only a house" Ibid., 108.

p. 43, "lazy poems" Cisneros, "Do You Know Me," 79.

p. 44, "Sesame Street . . . warm and beautiful" Aranda, "On the Solitary Fate," 69.

p. 44, "lived, or witnessed . . ." Ibid., 64.

p. 45, "It's a circular thing . . ." Ibid., 70.

CHAPTER FOUR: Crossing Borders

p. 46, "quite there" Cisneros, "Do You Know Me," 79.

p. 47, "that was that" Ibid.

p. 47, "the terror of . . . of a flashlight" Ibid.

p. 48, "women helped me . . ." Jussawalla and Dasenbrock, *Interview,* 298.

p. 49, "loose and deliberately . . . cuteness" "Review of *The House on Mango Street*, by Sandra Cisneros," *Booklist,* October 15, 1984, 28.

p. 50, "words to express . . ." Ibid.

p. 50, "foremost a storyteller" Gary Soto, "Voices of Sadness and Science," *The Bloomsbury Review*, July/August 1988, 21.

p. 51, "Elsewhere, poets . . ." Barbara Kingsolver, "Poetic Fiction with a Tex–Mex Tilt," *Los Angeles Times Book Review,* 28 April 1991.

p. 54, "trying to be . . ." Jussawalla and Dasenbrock, *Interview,* 299.

p. 55, "I had to be . . ." Aranda, "On the Solitary Fate," 70.

p. 56, "graceful two step . . . made me whole" Jussawalla and Dasenbrock, *Interview,* 291.

p. 57, "a home in the heart" Cisneros, *Mango Street,* 64.

CHAPTER FIVE: So Many Things Terrify
p. 59, "When I tried to translate . . ." Cisneros, *Mango Street,* 75.
p. 60, "wherever you put me . . . than the what" Jusswala and Dasenbrock, *Interview,* 291.
p. 60, "luxury . . ." Cisneros, "Ghosts," 73.
p. 61, "I would have to say . . ." Ibid.
p. 61, "I don't want to die . . ." Cisneros, "Notes," 76.
p. 62, "green card" Kathy Lowry, "The Purple Passion of Sandra Cisneros," *Texas Monthly,* vol. 25, no. 10, October 1997, 148-50.
p. 62, "redefining" Aranda, "On the Solitary Fate," 67.
p. 63, "They're a part of you . . ." Ibid.
p. 63, "I'm wearing . . . feminist be sexy" Ibid., 69.
p. 64, "Gentlemen, ladies . . ." Cisneros, *My Wicked Wicked Ways* (New York: Random House, 1987), ix.
p. 64, "the world of thousands . . . finally be heard" Cisneros, "Notes," 76.
p. 66, "wanderings . . ." Ibid., 74.
p. 66, "terrifying center" Aranda, "On the Solitary Fate," 75.
p. 62, "When you think . . ." Ibid., 75.
p. 66, "something someone wants . . ." Ibid., 76.

CHAPTER SIX: Fierce Women
p. 70, "The day Don Serafin . . ." Cisneros, *Woman Hollering Creek* (New York: Random House, 1991), 43.
p. 73, "You used to be . . ." Ibid., 89.
p. 74, "You remember . . ." Aranda, "On the Solitary Fate," 76.
p. 74, "fierce women . . ." Carmen Aguinaco, "Creative Tension: How Latina Writers Make Sense of Two Worlds," *U.S. Catholic,* November 1999, 35.
p. 75, "Human beings . . ." Cisneros, *Woman Hollering Creek,* 83.
p. 75, "Thank you . . . " Ibid., 124.
p. 75, "lit a candle . . ." Ibid., 121.
p. 75, "Can you please . . ." Ibid., 117.

p. 76, "real life . . ." Robin Ganz, "Sandra Cisneros: Border Crossings and Beyond," *Melus,* Spring 1994, 19-29.

p. 76, "Cuz you can relate . . ." Adria Bernardi, "*Woman Hollering Creek* Comes from the Heart," *Chicago Tribune: Woman News,* August 11, 1991, 12.

p. 76, "is written . . . first time" Ibid.

p. 76, "always sucking . . ." Aranda, "On the Solitary Fate," 77.

p. 77, "I read them . . . time gets stolen." Ibid.

p. 78, "I know there are . . ." Ganz, "Sandra Cisneros," 27.

p. 78, "fact that there's . . ." Don Swaim, interview with Sandra Cisneros, *Wired for Books,* CBS Radio Online, 1991, http:wiredforbooks.org/sandracisneros (accessed August 20, 2004).

p. 78, "literary" and "popular" Ibid.

p. 78, "use[s] reality . . . think so much, feel!" Ibid.

p. 83, "get on the track . . . right through you" Aranda, "On the Solitary Fate," 78.

CHAPTER SEVEN: Writer and Activist

p. 84, "help heal the pain" Benson, "From the Barrio to the Brownstone," F1.

p. 86, "a city of grief and pain" Jasna, "Letter from Sarajevo," *New York Times,* April 9, 1993, A12.

p. 87, "fearless . . . political content" Jusswala and Dasenbrock, *Interview,* 306.

p. 87, "San Antonio is where . . . in Spanish." Ibid., 288.

p. 91, "Sandranistas . . . publicity seeker" Lowry, "The Purple Passion," 148.

p. 91, "One day I'll own . . ." Cisneros, *Mango Street,* 87.

p. 92, "(1) at one time . . ." Lowry, "The Purple Passion," 149.

p. 94, "We are a people . . . the Tejano people" Ibid.

p. 95, "mail them to . . ." Ibid., 150.

p. 95, "with a magazine . . ." Ibid.

p. 96, "I don't know why . . ." Shoshanna Tenn, "Sandra Cisneros Saves the Color Purple," *Commonwealthclub.org,* 1992

archive, http://www.commonwealthclub.org/archives99/
cisneros.html (accessed April 21, 2002).

CHAPTER EIGHT: Keeping the Faith

p. 97, "to build self esteem . . ." Rohan B. Preston, "New YMCA
Center Backs Arts," *Chicago Tribune*, November 19, 1997,
Metro Section, 3.

p. 98, "hanging by my fingernails" Amy Goodman, *Democracy
Now,* Pacifica Radio Online, March 3, 1998,
www.webactive.com/webactive/pacifica/demnow/dn980303.html
(accessed April 4, 2002).

p. 99, "her pitch is . . ." Cassandra West, "Multimedia Listener's
Guide," *Chicago Tribune,* Sept. 13, 1998, Book Section, 8.

p. 100, "daughter of mexicanos . . . theater curtain." Cisneros,
Holler if You Hear Me, x.

p. 101, "It is a great . . ." Ibid., xii.

p. 101, "some Hispanics are charmed . . ." "Corrections and
Citations," *Chicago Tribune,* October 28, 1998, 3.

p. 101, "erroneous impression . . ." Ibid.

p. 102, "It was a great joy . . ." Tenn, "Sandra Cisneros Saves the
Color Purple."

p. 103, "Short of that step . . ." Cisneros, et al., "An Open Letter to
the President," *The New York Review of Books,* vol. 47, no.
20, Dec. 21, 2000, http://www.nybooks.com/articles/13937
(accessed August 20, 2004).

p. 104, "rat poor . . . certain richness" Robert Coles and Randy
Testa with Michael Coles, *Growing Up Poor: A Literary
Anthology* (New York: The New Press, 2001), 24.

p. 105, "Poetic, seemingly simple . . ." Patick T. Reardon, "Book
No. 2: Let the Debate Begin," *Chicago Tribune,* Oct. 17,
2001, "Tempo," 4.

p. 105, "people who are . . . evil out of your heart." Susan Latham,
"Author Sandra Cisneros Celebrates Day of the Dead," Nov.
2, 2001, http://journalism.berkeley.edu/students/latham/
cisneros.html (accessed April, 21, 2002).

p. 107, "It was apparent . . ." Arianne Schultheis, "Sandra Cisneros Plays with the Notion of Boundaries," *New University Newspaper* online, April 16, 2002, http://www.newu.uci.edu/archive/2001-2002/spring/020415/featstory04.htm (accessed August 20, 2004).

p. 108, "imagine what you say . . . an apprentice" Ibid.

p. 108, "sad . . . defeated . . . of my favorites" Patrick T. Reardon, "Escape from the City," *Chicago Tribune,* October 22, 2002, "Tempo," 1.

p. 110, "Sandra Cisneros has . . ." Valerie Sayers, "*Caramelo:* Traveling with Cousin Elvis," *New York Times Book Review,* September 29, 2002, 24.

p. 110, "to find the words . . ." Margaret Randall, "Weaving a Spell," *Women's Review of Books,* vol. 20, no. 1, October 2002, 1-2.

p. 113, "I've always thought . . ." Rene H. Shea, "Truth, Lies, and Memory: a Profile of Sandra Cisneros," *Poets and Writers,* September/October 2002, 34.

p. 115, "she felt impoverished . . ." Dianne Klein, "Coming of Age in Novels by Rudofo Anaya and Sandra Cisneros," *English Journal,* vol. 81, no. 5, September 1992, 21.

Bibliography

Aranda, Pilar E. Rodriguez. "On the Solitary Fate of Being Mexican, Female, Wicked and Thirty-three: An Interview with Sandra Cisneros." *The Americas Review,* vol. 19, no.1, Spring 1990, 64-80.

Brackett, Virginia. "Sandra Cisneros." *Encyclopedia of Catholic Literature.* Ed. Mary R. Reichardt. Westport, CT: Greenwood Publishing Group, 2004.

Cisneros, Sandra. *Caramelo.* New York: Alfred A. Knopf, 2002.

————."Do You Know Me? I Wrote *The House on Mango Street.*" *The Americas Review,* vol. 15, no. 1, Spring 1987, 77-79.

————. "Ghosts and Voices: Writing from Obsession." *The Americas Review,* vol. 15, no.1, Spring 1987, 69-73.

————. *The House on Mango Street.* New York: Random House, 1987.

————. *My Wicked Wicked Ways.* Berkeley, CA: Third Woman Press, 1987.

————. "Notes to a Young(er) Writer." *The Americas Review,* vol. 15, no. 1, Spring 1987, 74-76.

————. "Only Daughter." *Glamour,* November 1990, 256-258.

————. *Woman Hollering Creek.* New York: Random House, 1991.

Coles, Robert, and Randy Testa, with Michael Coles. *Growing Up Poor: A Literary Anthology.* New York: New Press, 2001.

Ganz, Robin. "Sandra Cisneros: Border Crossings and Beyond." *Melus* vol. 19, no. 1, Spring 1994, 19-29.

Jussawalla, Feroza, and Reed Way Dasenbrock. *Interview with Writers of the Post-Colonial World.* Jackson: University Press of Mississippi, 1992.

Klein, Dianne. "Coming of Age in Novels by Rudolfo Anaya and Sandra Cisneros." *English Journal,* vol. 81, no. 5, September 1992, 21-26.

Madsen, Deborah L. *Understanding Contemporary Chicana Literature.* Columbia: University of South Carolina Press, 2000.

Mirriam-Goldberg, Caryn. *Sandra Cisneros: Latina Writer and Activist.* Berkeley Heights, NJ: Enslow Press, 1998.

Mullen, Harryette Romell. "'A Silence Between us Like a Language': The Untranslatability of Experience in Sandra Cisneros's *Woman Hollering Creek.*" *Melus* 21 (Summer 1996): 3-20.

Olivares, Julian. "Entering *The House on Mango Street.*" *Teaching American Ethnic Literatures.* Ed. John R. Maitino and David R. Peck. Albuquerque: University of New Mexico Press, 1996.

Schultheis, Arianne. "Sandra Cisneros Plays with the Notion of Boundaries." The *New University* Newspaper, April 15, 2002. http://www.newuniversity.org/archive/2001-2002/spring/020415/featstory04.htm.

Swaim, Don. Interview with Sandra Cisneros. *Wired for Books,* CBS Radio Online, 1991, http://wiredforbooks.org/sandracisneros/

Index

Alexie, Sherman, 104
Alger, Horatio, 20
Anaya, Rudolfo, 82
Andersen, Hans Christian, 20

Bachelard, Gaston, 31
Bergholz, Susan, 62
Brooks, Gwendolyn, 37
Burton, Virginia Lee, 24
Bush, George W., 101-102, 104

Carver, Raymond, 11, 104
Castillo, Ana, 99
Cisneros, Elvira (mother), 14-
    16, 25
Cisneros, Sandra, *10, 93, 114*
    activism, 84-86, 103-104
    awards, 40, 55-56, 61-62,
        68, 86, 89
    Bad Boys, 38
    birth, 12
    Caramelo, 90, 102, 107,
        109-115, *111*
    education, 11-12, 22-24,
        25-33
    father's death, 90, 105-106
    Hairs/Pelitos, 87

*House on Mango Street,
    The,* 12, 21, 30, 32-33,
    38, 40, 42-45, 49-51,
    50, 57, 68, 78-79, 87,
    89, 91-92, 98-99, 104-
    105
    house-paint controversy,
        90-96
    Mexican heritage, 13-14,
        17-18, 21, 31-32, 34,
        45, 49, 54-55, 62-63,
        81, 87-88, 92-94, 101-
        102, 105-107, 115
    My Wicked Wicked Ways,
        38, 47, 61-66
    and relationships, 39-40, 65
    and teaching, 36-39, 57, 58-
        61, 76-77, 82-83
    Woman Hollering Creek,
        62, 68-77, 80-81
    and writing, 11-12, 19, 25-
        27, 30-35, 50-51, 59-
        61, 66-67, 82-83, 89,
        107-108
Cisneros del Moral, Alfredo (fa-
    ther), 13-15, 17, 27, 82, 90,
    105-106, 109

Clinton, Bill, 103-104
Cumpian, Carlos, 82

Day of the Dead, 105-106, *106*
de la Cruz, Sor Juana Inés, 99
Dickinson, Emily, 29, 33-34, 64
Didion, Joan, 103
Doctorow, E. L., 103
Dreiser, Theodore, 103

Ferber, Edna, 103
Forster, E. M., 99

Goodman, Amy, 98

Harjo, Joy, 33
Hinojosa, Maria, 95
Hughes, Langston, 104
Hurston, Zora Neale, 104

Iowa Writers' Workshop, 11-
  12, 29-33, 36, 45
Irving, John, 11

Justice, Donald, 29, 30

K., Jasna, 48, 85-86
Kanellos, Nick, 41, 46
Kingsolver, Barbara, 50-51
Kingston, Maxine Hong, 33, 87

Lee, Harper, 105
Leibovitz, Annie, 85
Little House, The, 24

Mamet, David, 103
Mathis, Dennis, 33, 41-42
Michie, Greg, 99-101
Morrison, Toni, 33

O'Connor, Flannery, 11

Pavlov, Ivan Petrovich, 22
Poetry Society of America, 37
Puig, Manuel, 87

Rodoreda, Mercè, 87
Rodriguez, Richard, 77
Rulfo, Juan, 87

Sandberg, Carl, 37
Silko, Leslie Marmon, 99
Sinclair, Upton, 103
Singer, Isaac Bashevis, 99
Soto, Gary, 38, 50, 77
Stegner, Wallace, 11
Styron, William, 103
Swaim, Don, 78-81

Vonnegut, Kurt, 103

Wright, Richard, 103

Zapata, Emiliano, 80-81, *80*